ML

CONTEMPORARY LATVIAN POETRY

IOWA TRANSLATIONS

General Editors
Hualing Nieh Engle
Paul Engle

CONTEMPORARY LATVIAN POETRY

Edited by
INARA CEDRINS

University of Iowa Press 🔱 Iowa City

Publication of this book was aided by a $3,000 grant from the Association for
the Advancement of Baltic Studies.

Library of Congress Cataloging in Publication Data
Main entry under title:

Contemporary Latvian poetry.

  (Iowa translations)
  Translated from Latvian.
    1. Latvian poetry—20th century—Translations into English.   2. English poetry—
Translations from Latvian.   I. Cedrins, Inara.   II. Series.
PG9145.E3C66   1984   891'.9313'08   84-8800
ISBN   0-87745-128-1   (pbk.)

University of Iowa Press, Iowa City 52242
© 1984 by The University of Iowa. All rights reserved
Printed in the United States of America

Errata

The following poems by Gunars Saliņš have been translated by the author:

"Lost in New York" (based on a translation by Ruth Speirs), page 31.
"Rain," page 39.
"Her Song on the Way to the Scaffold," page 45.
"Storm in the Streets" (based on a translation by Ruth Speirs), page 46.

In "Her Song on the Way to the Scaffold," page 45,
line 1 should read: "She approaches us along her song"
line 1, part II should read: "She sings again—."

CONTENTS

SOVIET LATVIAN POETS

FOREWORD

Translation is probably the least honored of all the arts, for it is indeed an art and not merely a technical skill. To understand the emotion in an image from another language and then to present it as a poem in a second language is a noble human act, only a little below the imaginative power which produced the original poem.

This is especially true when poems are translated from a language wholly obscure to most of the world, a language not usually taught in universities, almost never heard in the U.S.A. save among exiles, but of a rich texture and sonorous sound. Its obscurity, in a sense, makes translations from it more important than translations from the usual western languages which are, to an extent, known in this country; although the level of foreign language knowledge in our education is not only pitiful but dangerous.

Like so many small countries, and even some larger, Latvia has been invaded, massacred, suppressed, imprisoned, censored. Its poets, unlike poets in the West, have lived and written at the risk of their lives. American poets with their comfortable jobs and their complete freedom to write what they wish, have no experience of the invader, of the secret police watching their poetry, their correspondence (above all with foreign poets), and their friends. The poems in this book were written under political and social tensions western poets do not endure. In many countries under authoritarian governments, the lyrical expression of private emotions is regarded as a public betrayal, because it does not propagandize the government ideology.

The poets in this book are very brave as well as talented people. It is a sad commentary on the twentieth century that a poet should need to be courageous as well as gifted. The First World War proved that poets can be brave when fighting for their country in one of the great stupidities of this century, when poets on every side were fighting each other. But the new version of courage is for a poet to write his own individual verse.

It is crucial for the literature of these small, endangered countries to survive and to keep their poetry as well as their language alive, in the face of efforts to suppress their uniqueness and make them part of a mass conformation. The Finnish language has a wonderful word, "sisu," meaning, roughly, "endurance beyond endurance." The Latvians have it.

Translations of the Bible and Karl Marx have profoundly affected history. Turning the early Buddhist texts from intricate, polysyllabic Sanskrit into monosyllabic Chinese was not only one of the great intellectual triumphs of human life, it also profoundly changed Asian culture. Men and women lived differently because devoted translators gave them insights. More than ever it is true today—translate or die.

Hualing Nieh Engle
Paul Engle
International Writing Program
School of Letters
The University of Iowa

GENERAL EDITORS' ACKNOWLEDGMENTS

Many people of good will are behind this book in addition to the editor and translators. The International Writing Program has been from its beginning committed to the crucial importance of translation in these dark decades of the twentieth century when the peoples of the world must talk and understand each other in order to survive. Translation lights the darkness which separates us from each other.

It is heartening that many Iowa corporations and individuals support this view with their contributions: the Fred Maytag Family Foundation, Cedar Rapids *Gazette,* Des Moines *Register,* Ruan Transportation, American Republic Insurance, Employer's Mutual, Amana Refrigeration, Meredith Foundation, Grain Processing, Corp., Rockwell International, Dial Foundation, Bankers Life, Peter Bezanson, First National Bank (Iowa City), William Shuttleworth, and Clare Rice.

The University of Iowa has been deeply supportive. Its administrators have believed in all of the arts, of which translation is one. The first Translation Workshop in this country was established here. This University was the first in the U.S.A. (in the world?) to state in its catalog that creative work would be accepted as a dissertation for advanced degrees. "A contribution to knowledge" had been the usual phrase, but here an act of the imagination was also acceptable.

These members of the University have helped: James O. Freedman, president; Duane Spriestersbach, graduate dean; Richard D. Remington, vice president; Howard Laster, dean of liberal arts; Philip G. Hubbard, dean of academic affairs; Fredrick Woodard, associate dean of faculties; Richard Lloyd-Jones, chair, English. They believe and they act.

The United States Information Agency and Cultural Affairs Officers at American Embassies all over the world have from the beginning of this program eighteen years ago given grants to talented and published writers to come here and introduce the literature of their many languages to each other and to readers in this country. It is heartening to find our government willing to provide funds for the least dramatic and most private of all the arts—writing. Plays can be staged, compositions performed by orchestras, paintings and sculpture can be exhibited, dancers can show their marvelous motions to audiences. The writer sits alone moving words into forms which move readers. The translator also has his solitary art, but in some ways his job is quite as hard as that of the original writer, for he must draw words out of one language into another, yet he must recreate the original creation, making the second language as moving as the first. It is an act of submission. That a public agency of this country, the USIA, recognizes this skill is quite wonderful.

The International Writing Program and the University of Iowa Press have already published anthologies of poetry from Japanese, Korean, Chinese, Russian, and the languages of Yugoslavia and Romania in our Iowa Translations. It is important that the lyrical voices of little countries be heard in this age of big voices. It is also important that our unique combination of university, corporations, foundations, and the United States Information Service (with the invaluable help of Ruth Skartvedt over many years) makes possible such publications. W. Averell Harriman, our greatest statesman, helps us. We do not know of any other such group of such good will.

The University of Iowa Foundation gives indispensable support to all projects of the International Writing Program. They join our contributors who make washing machines, produce oil, design communications equipment for the moon capsule, and sell refrigerators and insurance in our practical way of bringing the imaginative poetry of other languages into imaginative English.

SWEDEN

HELSINKI

STOCKHOLM

TALLINN

ESTONIA

LATVIA

RIGA

LIEPAJA

BALTIC
SEA

LITHUANIA

VILNIUS

GDANSK

GERMANY

POLAND

BERLIN

WARSZAWA

100 50 0 100 200 300 400 500

THE BALTIC STATES

Juris Silenieks

INTRODUCTION

"For many centuries, while kingdoms rose and fell along the shores of
the Mediterranean and countless generations handed down their re-
fined pleasures and vices, my native land was a virgin forest whose only
visitors were the few Viking ships that landed on the coast,"[1] writes
Nobel Prize Laureate Czeslaw Milosz, born in Lithuania, a country with
which Latvia shares not only a common border but also a linguistic
heritage and a good deal of destiny's allotment of bad luck. And indeed,
until the thirteenth century, Amberland (a poetic name sometimes
given to Latvia) was forgotten. But once noticed, the Baltic region be-
came an object of conquest and colonization. The region has never
ceased to be invaded, partitioned, dismembered, oppressed, and brutal-
ized, since it is at the crossroads between the East and the West where
many nations have met and contested their claims. And if so far the
Latvians, together with their northern neighbors, Estonians, and Lith-
uanians to the south, have escaped total annihilation, their survival can
very well be attributed to the absurdities of fate, with chance and neces-
sity, as Jacques Monod argued, pursuing their enigmatic interplays
where the dour doggedness of the people and the ineptitudes of the
conqueror have also their parts.

The recent fate of the Baltic states can be quite instructive, prefigur-
ing so many subsequent developments in our century. Milosz notes that
in August 1939 the pact between Hitler and Stalin determined zones of
influence, whereby the three independent Baltic states fell, by the
agreement of the two leaders, under the Soviet regime.[2] Those leaders
are gone, but the world has accepted their legacy. A similar fate, in spite
of pious declarations on the rights of man and principles of self-
determination of nations, has befallen many other peoples.

An Historical Overview

Along this tortuous and tragic path of Latvian history, there are few
periods of peace and prosperity. Most frequently, this small plot of some
25,000 square miles, where the Latvians have been living for about three
thousand years, has been visited by wars, famines, plagues, military con-

quests, political subjugation, and cultural oppression. Recorded history of Latvia begins in the thirteenth century with the conquest of the Latvian tribes by German bishops and the Teutonic Order. From this time until 1918, when Latvia became independent, the Latvians were under dominance by a foreign power that always treated the land and its people as a colony, good for exploitation only.

Among the overlords, the Swedes alone are popularly remembered as having had a just and kind king. He would receive the peasants' petitions brought to him in wintertime by messengers crossing the frozen Baltic Sea on foot. Another bright interlude came with the Duchy of Courland under the rule of Duke Jacob, who brought peace and prosperity with his efforts to develop trade and industry, together with the acquisition of overseas lands in Gambia and Tobago. Except for these two periods of relative calm and justice, the seven hundred years of foreign rule signify misery and darkness for the Latvian people. The rural population was reduced to serfdom; in the cities the Latvians were restricted to small crafts, trade, and domestic service. An unusual linguistic phenomenon occurred: instead of accepting the conqueror's language, the Latvian peasant forced the German baron to learn his language in order to communicate. Since education was considered to be harmful to the serf's mentality, the people remained illiterate. Nevertheless, folk art and traditions persisted, and the creation of the rich corpus of Latvian folk songs (*dainas*) dates for the most part from these years of serfdom.

Thus, when in the middle of the nineteenth century Europe saw a wave of national movements, the Baltic region was considered as a colony, without its own culture, without its own ethnic identity. A Latvian was a peasant, and a peasant was a Latvian. An educated Latvian was simply a contradiction in terms. Those ambitious Latvians who managed to become educated and who occupied professional positions were quickly absorbed into the predominantly German cultural environment. Politically, however, Latvia was part of Russia. In the long-range political perspective, the Latvian seems to have always debated whether to fear the brutal embrace of the Russian bear more than the gifts of the German colonizer. Only once, immediately after World War I, did the Latvians succeed in taking advantage of the unresolved dispute between their big neighbors to accede to their own independent state. But to reach that stage when a people is sufficiently united and conscious of its own ethnic identity, years of struggle and maturation are needed.

The beginnings of national consciousness go back to the middle of the nineteenth century, when through hard work and patience a Latvian middle class was emerging in the cities, and the former serfs were finally permitted to acquire their homesteads. With the upward economic movement came a demand for equality of opportunity and equality before the law. The first educated Latvians began to assert their ethnic origins. The urban middle class demanded participation in city governance. The first cultural organizations were founded, and therewith came the beginnings of authentic Latvian literature.

Along with the national awakening came aspirations for a more autonomous state. There was resentment against the oppressive regime of the czars as well as against the tutelage of the German barons who, ever since their arrival in the region some seven centuries previously, served as spokesmen for the Latvian masses. In most instances they promoted their own interests and misrepresented the wishes of their constituency. Nationalism, which was a grass roots movement, and Marxism, recently imported from Western Europe, became rival ideologies vying for popular support, but they were united in their opposition to the czarist oppression and the exploitation by the German barons. Many intellectuals and writers who criticized the regime, or were suspected of criticizing it, were arrested and deported. Many others chose exile.

The 1905 Revolution in Russia had its own local dynamics in Latvia. The workers' strikes in the cities and the burning of the German barons' estates in the countryside were manifestations of the same pent-up rage and thirst for retribution that had conditioned Latvian sensitivities for centuries. In response to the outbreaks of disorder and violence, the czar sent a special punitive expedition that summarily executed revolutionaries and suspects. The aftermath of the 1905 Revolution occasioned another wave of involuntary emigration from Latvia and even tighter surveillance of nationalist aspirations. But it was not until 1918, following the collapse of Czarist Russia and the defeat of the German armies, that Latvia was proclaimed independent, with the support of the Allies. Yet it took the Latvian army more than a year to clear the territory of foreign occupants, the Red Army, and the remnants of the German Imperial Army.

The task of reconstruction in a country devastated by the war was equally onerous. A land reform program parceled and distributed the large estates owned by German barons to many sharecroppers and farm workers whose age-old dream to own a plot of land was finally realized. But the nation-building process also encountered many impediments. Among other things, the Latvian electoral law did not foster stable coalition governments, and political fragmentation was rampant. In 1934 Prime Minister Kārlis Ulmanis prepared a draft for a new constitution, but debates and amendments in the parliament promised little success. On May 15, 1934, Ulmanis engineered a coup and suspended the constitution. With unflagging energy he pursued a program of reconstruction that included institution of many American practices he had observed during his stay in the United States. Ulmanis's rule, however, was brief. Europe was in the throes of apocalyptic changes. The 1939 treaty between Germany and the Soviet Union left the Baltic States to the Soviets. German nationals were repatriated, and in June 1940 Stalin ordered the occupation of the three Baltic States. With adroit manipulation of electoral laws, a new parliament was elected that requested the Soviet Union to accept Latvia as one of the Soviet republics. Executions and deportations of political and military leaders and the intelligentsia followed. Less than a year later, before Stalin was able to implement fully his genocidal policies, the German armies overran the country. In their wake came political suppression, economic exploitation, and depletion of human resources through conscription, arrests, executions, and detention in concentration camps. With the retreat of the German armies in 1944 and the advance of the Red Army, the Latvians, as so many times before in history, were again caught between contending forces. Some chose exile voluntarily; some were simply swept along with the fleeing Germans; some opted for a guerrilla existence in the deep forests of Latvia; but most refused to leave the homeland.

It is estimated that some 200,000 Latvians sought refuge in the Western countries. Those who reached Germany were settled, after the conclusion of hostilities, in Displaced Persons' camps. From there, many emigrated to Australia, England, New Zealand, and Canada. With the passage of a special Displaced Persons Act by Congress, some 37,500 Latvians came to the United States. There are also sizable immigrant groups in Sweden, Germany, and elsewhere who identify themselves as

Latvians. In addition to the national language, there may be some other discernible ethnic characteristics that historians and sociologists seek to appraise and poets to evoke in their works. Both history and geography have left their imprint on the collective psyche of the inhabitants of Amberland.

Traits of the Latvian Ethos

Survival in Amberland has always been difficult, not only because of external political threats but also because of the physical environment. There is very little naturally rich soil, which is preponderantly diluvian and demands constant cultivation and fertilization. The challenge of the Baltic Sea and the unending contest with the elements have bred a strain of tenacity, a melange of optimism and stubbornness in the Latvian. Practicality and respect for the work ethic have permitted survival of Latvians, even if the luck of history has been against them. But the national psyche has its paradoxes and contradictions too. Though generally affirmative realists and enterprising individualists, the Latvians are subject to moods of lyric melancholy, inspired perhaps by the Nordic landscape. It is frequently enveloped in dense mists, and vegetation looks precarious and precious during the short, intense growing season. The winter nights are long and dark; the harsh winds inimical to human effort. There are constant challenges and threatening forces in nature as well as a promise of happiness and moments of epiphany. Next to this attraction to romantic melancholy, the Latvian harbors a sense of humor that often turns into caustic irony, so evident in the folk tales, songs, and proverbs.

The social unit that perhaps has played the most important role thoughout Latvian history is the family. The operations of individual farmsteads required respect for the authority that was vested in the head of the household. In this agrarian society, women, who generally achieved the status of companion to their mates, were equally important as the educators of the young and the guardians of beauty and harmony. They, too, have preserved "some of that ancient sadness which is a sort of pride with defenseless yet highly self-conscious small nations."[3]

In our times of accelerated changes and transformations, an assessment of national characteristics of this kind is, of course, almost impossible, and not as relevant as some sociologists contend. Perhaps the

Latvian type described above is no longer extant; perhaps it has never existed as a type. But as an ideal, as an image, it is likely to be recognized as Latvian *grosso modo* and very much present in Latvian poetry. Of course, the key indicator of national identity is language.

The Latvian Language

Although much uncertainty and contention still surround ethnogenetic questions of the Baltic language group, certain historicolinguistic points are well established. "Latvian is a very old language," is a statement often heard. From the historicolinguistic point of view, remarks of this kind are true only in a certain sense. For example, in the Romance language group, which probably has the most complete historical records, the major languages, French, Spanish, Italian, and Portuguese, all trace their origins back to Latin. In other words, during the course of many centuries, Latin evolved into the contemporary Romance languages. To say that French or Spanish is an old language may not signify much, but they are contemporary representatives of Latin, which has ceased to exist as a "living" language. The conservative character of Latvian, however, makes it comparable to Latin and Greek.

Latvian and Lithuanian form the two extant Baltic languages in the Indo-European group. The ur-language of the group is called Proto-Indo-European, from which Proto-Baltic, along with Proto-Italic, Proto-Indo-Iranian, and others evolved. Proto-Baltic, in turn, has two branches: Proto-East-Baltic and Proto-West-Baltic. West-Baltic is represented by Old Prussian, extinct today. East-Baltic is split into four groups: two extant, Latvian and Lithuanian, and two extinct, Selonian and Semigallian. Between the two groups there is also the extinct Curonian.

A considerable debate evolves around the special, apparently symbiotic, relationship of Baltic and Slavic languages, since both groups are very conservative, were recorded at a relatively late date, and have been neighbors for many centuries. But they have never been identical, and from the point of view of linguistic taxonomy the two groups are not to be lumped together.

As some linguists insist, this scheme is oversimplified. Yet it is generally agreed that the Baltic languages appear to have undergone fewer changes than any other Indo-European language group. Closely behind

Lithuanian, the Latvian language has preserved phonemic features that charaterized the Proto-Indo-European language but have been lost in most other present Indo-European languages. Though generally discredited by knowledgeable linguists, one story holds that a scholar of Sanskrit (the most important literary language of India, going back to 1000 B.C., and also of Proto-Indo-European provenance) was able to converse with a peasant while traveling through Lithuania. It is true, however, that because of the similarities in the morphological structure of nouns and verb conjugations, for example, a knowledge of Baltic is important for comparative Indo-European and historical Slavic studies.[4]

The Latvian alphabet, including long and short vowels and palatalized consonants, has thirty-four characters. Pronunciation is quite phonetic. Latvian has tone, as in Lithuanian, Norwegian, or Chinese. It is a highly inflected language, and stress occurs on the first syllable.[5]

It is generally thought that Latvian is a difficult language and that only those born into it can fully master its complexities. There are of course exceptions. But actually Latvian as a literary language begins only with the first native writer, all previous efforts having significance solely as historical documents.

The Balts appear on the historical scene with the mention of Aistians (i.e., speakers of Baltic languages) in Tacitus' *Germania,* ch. XLV. The earliest records of anything written in Latvian date from the thirteenth century. The first book written in Latvia, but not in the Latvian language, is *Origines Livoniae* by Henry of Livonia about 1220. Literary Latvian, in a restricted sense, starts with the post-Reformation period in the sixteenth century. The oldest surviving printed text in Latvian is Johann Hasentoter's script of the Lord's Prayer printed in 1550. The oldest surviving printed book is a Catholic catechism dating from 1585, followed by the New Testament in 1685 and the Old Testament in 1689. The language of the *Bible* was the mode and the model used by all authors in the seventeenth and eighteenth centuries. Writing in Latvian fell at that time to well-meaning German pastors who did not master the language and who, for the most part, considered it a peasant vernacular, useful for religious purposes and adequate for simple domestic life.

The next important stage in the development of the Latvian language came in the middle of the nineteenth century with the National Awakening movement. A poetry book entitled *Dziesmiņas* (Little Songs), by

Juris Alunāns in 1856, marks the beginning of indigenous Latvian literature proper. This first attempt was modest enough, containing translations of poems of world literature and a short note on the Latvian language. The book was printed in Gothic type. In the wake of Alunāns's humble effort came a generation of intellectuals and writers who saw it as their responsibility to develop Latvian into a modern language, capable of serving as a means of communication and artistic expression of subtlety and forcefulness. New words were coined, and initial efforts to codify the language and purify it from unwanted foreign influences were launched. These activities reached their peak during the period 1918–40, when Latvian was the language of sovereignty. Among the linguists, the most eminent place befalls Jānis Endzelīns, whose treatise on Latvian grammar and phonetics is a bench mark in the development of modern linguistics. Along with Russian, Latvian is still the official language of the Latvian Soviet Socialist Republic, now spoken by less than 55 percent of its population, or some 1.5 million people. It is constantly menaced by extinction because of the prevalence of the all-powerful Russian language. Latvian is the first language for minority groups in the United States, Australia, England, Canada, Germany, Sweden, and other countries. The retention rate of the native tongue among Latvian emigres is 50 percent, a rate considered by sociologists as being well above the average among American immigrants. Yet the prospects for the survival of Latvian outside the country are dim, and even its continued existence on its own soil is highly precarious.

Nationalism and Soviet Ideology

In the Soviet state, the question of nationalism and national culture has been subject to policies that are often ambiguous and contradictory. Somehow, the Stalin dictum regarding national literatures, "socialist in content and national in form," could never be consistently realized as a provisional expedient during the elaboration of the ultimate universal proletarian culture of the *homo sovieticus.* Internal and external crises have forced the rulers to execute ideological about-faces that sometimes suggest leniency, but more often intransigence toward nationalism, which is generally considered an execrable leftover of bourgeois mentality. Sometimes during periods of literary regimentation the Latvian writer has been urged to look for guidance and inspiration to Russian literature, whose anointed writers, experienced in the modes of socialist writing, can serve as models. More recently, Brezhnev's statement on the sixtieth anniversary of the Bolshevik Revolution that "the nationality question has been settled completely, finally and for good," has an ominous ring to the Latvians.

The concerns of the Latvian writer about Latvian cultural identity and survival are these days heightened by disquieting demographic and economic developments. The indigenous population, as compared with non-Latvians, is steadily declining because of the influx of Russian migrants and the decline in Latvian population growth. The cultural corollary is the increasing prevalence of Russian as the official as well as the most practiced language. The threat to the national culture is perceived as a dire reality. Large industries in rural and urban centers are attracting labor from other republics, thereby creating towns of considerable size with virtually no Latvian inhabitants. Russification of school curricula goes on unabated. According to a recent report, the number of hours of Russian studies has been increased.[6] Teacher and student meetings are conducted in Russian. Intermarriages of Russians and Latvians are encouraged, and theater repertories and concert programs must have a certain proportion of Russian works.

One of the first direct manifestations of protest against this cultural imperialism came with an open letter sent by seventeen Latvian members of the Communist party to several Communist parties in the West.[7] In literature, pleas for ethnic tolerance are couched in more cautious terms. But the "Defense and Illustration of the Latvian Language," to paraphrase the title of the sixteenth century work by Humanist Joachim Du Bellay that laid one of the cornerstones of French literature, is written and rewritten today in many forms. The difference is that French Renaissance writers tried to upgrade the French language to the level of the most cultured languages, while Latvian writers are engaged in a struggle for national survival.

The Role of the Poet

The precariousness of the Latvian language is not only a thematic preoccupation in Latvian literature; it also gives special significance to publishing. The publication of a work by a well-known author is an event awaited with anticipation and even anxiousness, since Soviet book printing quotas are not based on demand and it is not always possible to obtain the desired book. To a degree this bibliophilia is attributable to the reverence with which Latvians treat their writers, especially their poets. The Latvian poet in Soviet Latvia enjoys what is perhaps a legacy of the national past, the romantic notion, à la Victor Hugo, that projects the poet figure as the prophet, the sage, the leader of the people. The National Awakening movement in the nineteenth century was launched and spearheaded by intellectuals of poetic bent and success. The most prominent personage of this mold is Jānis Rainis, a poet of classical inclination, who by popular and critical consensus is Latvia's greatest poet. Before World War I, he spent many years in prison and in exile for his activities promoting the idea of national independence. Upon return to independent Latvia, he assumed important administrative posts, thus exemplifying with his life and literary work the committed poet.

It is in times of hardship and uncertainty that the people look up to the poet for moral strength, spiritual guidance, and encouragement. In an outburst of anger, Hemingway once remarked to a Soviet critic: "A writer is like a Gypsy. He owes no allegiance to any government. If he is a good writer, he will never like the government he lives under." The Soviet Latvian poet, of course, has to tread more cautiously in order to see his poetry in print. There may be an occasional hosanna to the powers that be, but there is no deviation from his allegiance to the people. Echoing Pablo Neruda's statement, the Latvian poet Plaudis says: "The poet belongs to the world: first of all to his people and the country with the riches and values they have created, to the land that feeds him; after this—to other peoples and countries with the values they have created and which enrich his country and his people."[8]

Czeslaw Milosz evokes another reason for the admiration poets in Eastern Europe enjoy: "In our part of Europe, a poet is a preserver of pure language, language which is being distorted by mass media. . . . Preservation of a pure language and preservation of freedom, a word so often used although the people who use it very rarely understand the weight and the value of that word, that is the role of the poet."[9]

The Latvian language is thus in double jeopardy, being prone, like any other living language, to lose its internal cohesiveness. It is assailed by disruptive forces that operate within our societies, and it is subject to external pressures of assimilation, arising from its geopolitical situation. The minority's struggle for survival is likely to precipitate a heightened linguistic consciousness, since language is after all the most precious possession of an ethnic collectivity. In the face of changes in the total cultural environment, coupled with socioeconomic adjustments caused by industrialization and urbanization, linguistic conservatism is an unacceptable alternative, since language, too, is a living organism and must change with its environment. But the concomitant with change is frequently a degradation of usage, a degeneracy of linguistic sensibilities, attraction to cliché, platitude, the easy word. Thus, it is the poet's *raison d'être*, his incumbency and inner necessity, both to preserve language and ever to renew it through his poetic gift, which gives back to the word its meaning, its power of incantation.

An Historical Overview of Latvian Folk Songs and Literature

In one of his more morose moods, Andrejs Upĩtis, a Soviet Latvian poet and critic of considerable repute and controversy, once declared that "by his very nature, every Latvian poet is condemned to love his people."[10] And true enough, nationalism was the initial impetus that gave rise to Latvian literature, and it has been Latvian literature's essence, for better or for worse. Though properly speaking the starting point of indigenous Latvian literature is the publication of a collection of poetry in 1856, Latvian poetic traditions are deeply rooted in the folk songs (*dainas*), whose origins go back to the darkest days of serfdom.

The *dainas* form a huge corpus of songs, most typically quatrains, some two million in number with the inclusion of variants. Their collection and classification were the life-long effort of a dedicated folklorist, Krišjānis Barons. The *dainas* are a rich source of all kinds of ethnographic and anthropological information about the daily life, social relations, rituals and warfare, myths and beliefs, and values of an agrarian culture developing in a region where the climate is moderate, where the soil sustains only those who work hard, and where the landscape, crisscrossed and dotted by lakes and rivers, verdant with meadows, fields, forests, and groves, offers lyrical beauties. Thus, most predominantly, the *dainas* celebrate nature, which is the fount of human strength, wisdom, and goodness; they emphasize man's need to live in conformity with its laws. Among the values most highly praised are respect for life and the natural world, patience and moderation, industriousness and generosity. Mingled with the joys of life is a measure of melancholy and resignation that comes from the recognition of ineluctable fate, which metes out reward and punishment not always in conformity with man's sense of justice. There are also *dainas* of social protest, inveighing against the miseries of serfdom: the tortures of the threshing barn where labor for the feudal lord saps strength from the body and color from the cheeks. The expression, however, is highly restrained and very laconic, close to what McLuhan would designate as a "cool" style of communication. To a large degree, the *dainas* represent the summation of the Latvian ethos. They were sung daily, in the house as well as in the yard and in the fields, accompanying the Latvian through the rites of passage from birth to death. The *dainas* observe very distinct patterns of versification. To use the traditional terminology, which modern investigators have found inadequate and irrelevant, there are three distinct verse forms: trochee, dactyl, and asymmetric verse. The typical stanza is the quatrain.[11]

Though daily recitation of *dainas* is no longer practiced, the Latvians, especially those of the older generation, having studied them in school and heard them in concerts and recitals, are truly imbued with their spirit and rhythms. Conscious of this great folkloric treasure, Latvian poets have always attempted to use folk meter in their verse, though with varying success. The romantic appeal of a native art meter was especially strong during the National Awakening movement. These efforts, however, produced no significant results, mostly because, as modern linguists have pointed out, they lacked an adequate conceptual framework. It was only the talented poet with a highly intuitive grasp, like Jānis Rainis, who could successfully utilize folk meter in his verse. Yet *dainas,* in either form or spirit, seem to be an elemental ingredient of the Latvian poet's sensibility. The contemporary generation of poets, both in Latvia and outside, no longer tries to borrow directly from the *dainas,* recognizing their inimitable character. Most frequently, a poet may use a phrase or a line for contrast or mood, or a parodied expression for comic effect, as if through this atavism the present were to be made to appear illogical or ridiculous. As some scholars have pointed out, the *dainas* offer a kind of antidote to the contemporary "hot" line, be it capitalist advertising or communist propaganda slogans.[12]

Compared to the preliterate period of the *dainas,* the history of written Latvian poetry is relatively brief. Its beginnings coincide with the national aspirations toward political autonomy that were gaining momentum in the middle of the nineteenth century. By that time, European literatures had already embraced and abandoned Classicism, Romanticism, Realism, and other movements, and were ready for Impressionism and Symbolism. The catching-up of the newborn Latvian literature is marked by diversity and by a strange synchronic confluence of aesthetic tendencies that in other literatures follow a diachronic order. Thus, classical forms are evident in the works of Jānis Rainis. Romantic penchants inform the poetry of his life-long companion Aspāzija, as well as the verse of many other contemporaries. The plays of Rūdolfs Blaumanis, one of the first Latvian playwrights of note, are fashioned after the realist models. Furthermore, the commitment by most major literary figures of the period to the realization of the dream of independence gave their works a distinctly nationalistic orientation.

The late twenties and the early thirties saw a surge of new sensibilities with modernist penchants. Among the iconoclasts who were reluctant to toe the line of nationalist ideology is Aleksandrs Čaks (1901–50). He avowed affinities with poets of many stripes, such as Villon, Byron, Baudelaire, Mayakovsky, and Pasternak. A kind of Latvian *poète maudit,* Čaks was accused of tavern psychology and hooligan ideology by the straitlaced. Giving free rein to his attraction to erotica, to "chosisme," to the deviant from the norm, he was searching for an existence of multiple facets. In form, he frequently abandoned traditional patterns of versification, preferring rhythm over rhyme. Čaks continued to write and sometimes to publish, not always unscathed, and he managed to survive three political regimes: the independence period, the Russian takeover of 1940, the German occupation, and the return of the Russians in 1945. Most of the Latvian poets of the contemporary generation, both in Latvia and in exile, avow their indebtedness to Aleksandrs Čaks.

Poets outside Latvia

As one may expect, exile occasioned prodigious amounts of writing. There were those who felt it their sacred duty to redress the national wrongs, and their work exemplifies writing for political purposes. But exile also inspired writing that goes beyond the limits of political commitment. While the national bards continued to turn out patriotic verse, a new generation of poets came of age in the late fifties and early sixties, most of them members of a circle that took its name, "Hell's Kitchen," from the Manhattan neighborhood of artists and immigrants where these poets would gather. Of the six exile poets included in the present volume, Bičole, Kraujiete, Saliņš, and Tauns were members of "Hell's Kitchen." Ivaska and Stumbrs were not, yet their verse shares certain general characteristics with the poets of "Hell's Kitchen." All six were born in Latvia, where they received their primary and secondary education, and left their homeland before publishing a major work. The rigors of the Latvian school curriculum, ethnocentric in its ideological orientation and disciplinarian in its methodological approach, gave them a solid foundation in Latvian culture and letters. Most of them continued their education in Western European and American universities, thereby coming in contact with cosmopolitan crosscurrents as well as acquiring proficiency in English. They frequently translate their own verse into English or English poetry into Latvian, and some of their poems are originally written in English. In a way, this cultural pluralism and bilingualism tempers the trauma of war and exile.

Unlike the emotion-drenched pathos of the poetry of the patriotic bards, the apolitical and polysemous poetry of this group shuns gesture and pose and abstains from the angularities of committed writing. Nevertheless, the verse is informed by an authentic Latvian ethos and is very much rooted in the national heritage. As in a Bartók string quartet where the familiar Hungarian airs are invested with new tonal dynamics, there are resonances from *dainas,* an ancient motif interwoven in a modern texture, echoes of folkloric rhythms mixing with contemporary syncopes. Sharing affinities with the prewar modernist Čaks, this verse generally eschews the time-honored devices of versification in preference for an irregular line, short and intense, without rhyme, "ce bijou d'un sou," as Verlaine so contemptuously put it. The group's iconoclasm is not the result of a gratuitous quest for originality, but rather a sign of nonconfidence in the forms that once conveyed a vision of the world. As Yves Bonnefoy, discussing classical prosody and free verse, stated: "The conventions in the prosody were . . . in themselves the *metaphor* of the social law. . . . And the beauty of at least many poems in this frame reflected the fact that this law was one and alive: that man participated happily in a common meaningful order."[13] This order, once based on a system of logocentric metaphysics, is no longer ours. The word, corroded by political slogans and advertising jingles, and overused in a society given to logorrhea, no longer guarantees a preordained meaning. Thus, the poetry of the six can be viewed as an attempt to rescue language from meaninglessness as well as to give "Latvianness" a new dimension of relevance. Beyond this paradigm of general cultural determinants and biographical accidents, the six poets residing outside Latvia offer a range of idiosyncratic differences.

Linards Tauns (1922–63), can be considered as first among equals. He is basically an urban poet, pulsating with the restless rhythms of the big city, fascinated by the ethnic confluence and linguistic babel of New York. Beyond New York, there are the distant northern city of Riga and the ancient Mediterranean Rome, encompassed in a vision that transcends time, space, and causality to capture the transitory and the eternal, the profane and the sacred, the trivial and the tragic. The present projects toward an apocalyptic future and extends back into the past, which is not merely recollected but relived. A street scene, a prostitute in a tavern, a child playing with a balloon, a dog before the city gates, seized in privileged moments of consciousness, come forth as epiphanies. These moments of heightened being, as if triggered by sudden illuminations when the truth itself is revealed, bring forth beauty and a kind of inner closeness with and total apprehension of the world. The visionary and the saint, of course, cohabit with the bohemian and the hedonist, and the epiphanies give way to the miseries and loneliness of exile. The man-made world sometimes elicits a secret longing for the calm and harmony of nature, as if an ancestral strain in the Latvian psyche had suddenly surfaced. Tauns died too early to leave a following of disciples, but poetic cross-fertilization is a manifest legacy of his poetry among his fellow poets of "Hell's Kitchen."

Gunārs Saliņš is likewise a latter-day urban poet, urbane, witty, with a sense of earnestness and irony. His verse is carefully sculpted to convey impressions of naturalness and ease. Sound and meaning are welded together with the skills of a craftsman and a magician who know how to unlock the poetic secrets of language. The rhythms of Saliņš' verse suggest combinations of folkloric patterns with jazz inflections and nervous contemporary beats, finely attuned to the sounds of New York.

Echoes of Latvian rural sonorities mix with New York's din and bustle. An ironic refrain, an irreverent tra-la-la, jingling, hollow-sounding colloquialisms, and slang sometimes muffle the deep assonances of the poignancy of exile, the existential anguish before the irreducible absurdities of life. There is also in the modern urbanite an irrepressible rural romantic. Sometimes, as if yielding to some compulsive atavism, Saliņš invests the city scene with bucolic signs of vernal regeneration and rejoicing. Saliņš's latest collection of verse, *Satikšanās* [Encounter], is a travelogue of sorts. It records his impressions of Europe and of his return to Latvia, and adds new facets to his first volumes. It is an encounter with the old, rediscovered and overlaid with new significations that only wisdom, serenity, and authenticated sarcasm can gather from the experience of having lived with lucidity. There are also encounters that were expected to be with the past, with a former self perhaps, long lost in the business of continuing living. But the home left behind is unrecognizable, and what stares one in the face is mute suffering, absurdities of fate, mutilations of body and mind. Encounters with friends departed evoke the loss that accrues with time and death.

If Saliņš is primarily urban, abrasive and charming, with a penchant for irony and ambiguity, Baiba Bičole is most often reaching for a kind of "elementalism" in her encounter with the world. Exemplifying the Pound dictum that the natural object is the most adequate symbol, her verse is couched in a terse idiom, characterized by the naturalness of the noun and the forcefulness of the verb, dispensing with the finespun adjective and the oblique adverb. Her lines are short, rhymeless, without strophic divisions, since feeling is to gush forth uninterrupted. Sometimes the cascading typographical line arrangement makes the eye hurry, as if the intensity of feeling could not tolerate a moment of suspension. The magic of the word is fleeting, for, prolonged, it would diffuse into hollow rhetoric. Bičole's world is a plenum of four primary elements: water, fire, air, earth, in constant flux and interaction with the human body. The human body is the source of all emotion as it discovers the primeval forces of nature and experiences oneness with what is not mind. Bičole's exaltation over a union with the physical world intimates ancient fertility rites where the erotic and the sacred intermingle in ecstasy and mystery. But there are also pain and absence, faint reminders of the expulsion from paradise for the transgression of embracing the world. And with her later verse appear the self-inflicted tortures of the hedonist facing a diminishing world: "I am a nail in my own flesh."[14] "Daily, from me / a bucket is taken / Will I soon be empty?" (p. 82). If the poetic worlds of Saliņš and Bičole undergo transformations with the wear of time, Kraujiete's verse changes little.

Aina Kraujiete's verse is endowed with an intellectuality that is carefully balanced against the verse's emotional pull. For her, poetry is an exploration of multiple forms of being through empathy with other potential and actual facets of existence. The lunatic, the old lady whose present decrepitude hides past splendors, and the slum dweller of potentials unrealized are all projections of the same self seeking other ontological contours. For the most part, Kraujiete's verse is highly elliptical. The deliberate fragmentation of thought, the staccato rhythms, the obliqueness of the poetic statement require the reader's participation in filling the hiatuses, in rounding out the contours. Kraujiete's mood can be philsophical; her perspective tends toward the epic, the monumental, the mystical. Scenes of New York's glitter and triviality, culture and refinement interchange with sketches of Spanish Harlem. But the urbanist sometimes yields to romantic moods to rich fantasy that evokes the faraway land, the sadness of exile, the awareness of old age, the presence of death—a kind of ontological malaise that is the existential paradigm of modern man. Stumbrs, too, foreshadows some of these moods.

Olafs Stumbrs's poetry is multifaceted. Black humor and self-irony, as dampers on his inner emotional surge and as reactions to the social environment, blend with an existential anguish before man's essential solipsism and incommunicability, before life's passage toward degradation, old age, death. His occasional sarcasm betrays perhaps a deepseated need for love, gentleness, understanding. The social scene, obliquely humorous, is peopled with caricatures of types observed among his compatriots. The poet's beautiful descriptions of landscapes in accurate, realistic detail, sometimes evoke a trenchant melancholy, a nostalgia for the past so irretrievably lost in the vacuousness and vulgarity of the present. Stumbrs' poetry abounds in syntactical convolutions and elliptic thought—characteristics so often attributed to the exile's mentality.

As Mārtiņš Zīverts, one of the foremost Latvian playwrights, observed, Latvian literature in exile has no soil to grow roots in, while in Latvia it has no air to breathe. The expelled Russian poet Joseph Brodsky lamented that the exile poet quickly loses his linguistic roots by not hearing the language spoken by the people in taverns, buses, and grocery stores. That, of course, is the predicament of the Latvian exile poets—not to hear the language of the people in their own land, not to see it change, acquire new expressions, and undergo contaminations. In exile the processes diverge. While the typical immigrant gradually loses contact with the language, which is restricted to kitchen conversations replete with borrowings from the immediate linguistic environment, the poetic idiom, detached from the impurities of daily living, becomes more refined and ritualized. Such is the case with Astrīde Ivaska's poetry, the language of which seeks to distill the very essence of the Latvian linguistic heritage, or as Mallarmé intoned, to give "un sens plus pur aux mots de la tribu."

Ivaska's poetry is a celebration of the preciousness of language. Her verse brings out unsuspected lyric qualities whereby words become endowed with new meaning. This is perhaps an illustration of the structuralist notion that "words derive meaning not from any intrinsic value a word carries inside itself but from a double system of metaphor and metonymy that links words to each other and gives the words fleeting intelligibility rather than detached permanence." Ivaska creates new tonalities with subtle rhythms, new configurations of sounds through internal rhymes, echoes, palindromes, and alliterations. Her poetry opens to the world in many ways. The genesis of her poetic space starts with the contemplation of curtains, a dear memento from Riga. Now hung before the window in a new home, they filter the images received from the outside world. A spatial empathy develops with the Oklahoma landscape; a sympathetic resonance arises from the Finnish summer scene, or a Mediterranean seascape. The personal experience transcends the individual to acquire dimensions of universality and timelessness. In the face of the morosity of modern sensibilities, the poet pleads for affection, justice, respect for human dignity, and life. For both substance and form, Ivaska's poetry draws on *dainas*. Man's need to feel a closeness with nature, the source of beauty and truth, is a persistent motif modulated on occasional folkloric rhythms. As with some of the other exile poets, Ivaska's recent verse attains an ever greater density of thought and imagery, dropping delightful ornament in preference to opacity and intensity. Ivaska's preoccupations are shared by many other contemporary Latvian poets on both sides of the ideological divide.

Soviet Latvian Poets

The rapprochement across political boundaries that were to divide Latvian poetry proceeds from a sense of the common historical destiny. The Latvian cultural precariousness and the threat to the ethnic identity are concerns precipitated by the contemporary Latvian experience. The poets' response, regardless of the place of residence, has been a search for values in the national past and a cultivation of the Latvian language. There are, of course, significant differences between the situations of the exile poet and his Soviet Latvian counterpart. Perhaps first and foremost, the latter is to follow the precepts of socialist realism, not as much enforceable in poetry as in drama and prose, yet exacted nevertheless by the guardians of literary orthodoxy.

The definitions and interpretations of socialist realism, throughout the existence of the Soviet state, have shown subtle shifts of emphasis. One of the most characteristic pronouncements dates from the Zhdanov era.[15] It insists that socialist realism, a method of literature and literary criticism, be observed in depicting reality in its revolutionary development, with the intent to inoculate the masses with the spirit of socialism. Stalin's directive to the artist and the creative writer declared that realism is necessary and possible to the extent that it is deliberately socialistic. According to a popular quip, however, socialist realism is that brand of naturalism which is currently favored by the Central Committee.

During the difficult postwar years, socialist realism, as it was understood by its practitioners, engendered a great number of potboilers in prose fiction and grotesque hybrid forms of the well-made play in drama. As the structuralists aptly observe, every writer works in a tradition. The reader of a deserving work has a vivid awareness of two orders: the traditional canon and artistic novelty—a deviation from the canon. The hack and the journeyman take tradition for granted and crank out works according to formula. What the structuralists say about tradition can be applied legitimately to the norms that the Soviet writer is expected to observe. For the mediocre and the sycophant, the ideological prescriptions and proscriptions are welcome surrogates for originality. For the serious writer, censorship is a challenge that can stifle as well as stimulate creativity.

Total freedom in the arts and letters has not always occasioned a Golden Age of creativity and artistic perfection. Goethe's statement that only in constraint the true master proves himself is echoed in modern times by Borges's contention that censorship challenges the writer to make his point with ever greater care and subtlety. French Classicism flourished in an ambiance of conformity which brooked little deviation from what was quite narrowly defined to be true and beautiful by the legislators of the Parnassus. Jean-Paul Sartre alluded to the authenticity of literary effort under the German occupation of France. And some critics are of the opinion that Solzhenitsyn, now living in a world with freedom to burn, is no longer capable of attaining the intensity of thought and the beauty of expression that characterize his work written under Soviet censorship. That, of course, remains to be seen. The situation of contemporary Soviet Latvian literature poses challenges of equal magnitude, arising from adversity and from the literature's sense of mission.

Given the predicament of Soviet literature, the poet is in a more privileged position than the playwright and the novelist. While in prose, language functions primarily as a system of signs, in poetry it is the words that are apprehended. Poetry is more abstract and universal than prose, since its total signification is carried on many levels, beyond the mere semantic import of words. The language used in poetry exists, to a large extent, for itself, sufficient unto itself. One could argue that poetry is thus less vulnerable to the dictates of ideological regimentation. But the fluctuating fortunes of so many Soviet Latvian poets who have not escaped critical incrimination would not lend much support to such contentions. After all, a poem is not only an act of consciousness but also an expression of collective consciousness, particularly in the case of Soviet Latvian poets. And it may very well be the latter dimension that accounts for the popularity—in the best sense of the word, not mere faddish adulation—of Soviet Latvian poets.

Collective consciousness, as much as it may be decried by contemporary sociologists as a romantic notion, nevertheless is a preoccupation of writers who deal with collectivities subjected to alienation. The early

Marxist notion was that the proletariat, representing the alienated class in the reified capitalist world, would accede to a heightened form of self-consciousness, being the dynamic social group. George Lukacs, the celebrated Marxist critic and philosopher who fell into disgrace with the Soviet regime, notes that collective consciousness is a possible consciousness which men would have had if they had been able to grasp perfectly this situation and the benefits resulting from this situation.[16] Similarly, it could be argued, collective consciousness is a project that Soviet Latvian writers, members of a threatened and alienated people, seek to realize. A part of the project is to renew the Latvian's ties with the past in order to search for a new relevance of meaning in history. Pierre Henri Simon, in his analysis of the sensibilities of contemporary writers, notes: "What the writer today means by history is not, of course, a reconstitution, even if it were complete, of the past; it is the human becoming, in its total reach, past, present, and future, integrally bound as the very essence of the human adventure and sometimes the entire cosmic adventure."[17]

The tortured past has left scars in the Latvian psyche. Imants Auziņš, a poet of significant achievement and popularity, evokes scenes of the former conquerors and occupiers of the land: the Teutonic crusaders with wide shields and spears, the devastating hordes of Ivan the Terrible, the punitive expedition of General Sheremetev, the firing squads of the Czars—who all came to rape the land and enslave the people. Vizma Belševica, in her *chef d'oeuvre* of epic scope, "The Notations of Henry the Latvian on the Margins of the Livonian Chronicle," conjures up a haunting vision of the crucified land, the suffering of the people, the treason of the collaborators "with the obliging face," the imposition of "One God, one tongue"—evocations intended, undoubtedly, for the reader to probe their significance beyond the limits of historicity. There are also allusions to more recent history, to the early poets of the National Awakening movement, who were all marked by patriotism, and to the celebrated Latvian riflemen who, to a large extent shaped the national destinies. The allusions are reminders of the legacy of the national past.[18]

A Guyanese writer, Wilson Harris, referring to the significance of history in the process of nation building, calls for "a drama of consciousness which reads back through the shock of place and time for omens of

capacity, for thresholds of capacity that were latent."[19] The Soviet Lat-
vian poet also searches in the historical antecedent for a source of
strength for the present and a resolve for the future. Beyond these the-
matic preoccupations characterizing much of Soviet Latvian poetry to-
day, there is a variety of individual destinies, poetic penchants, and
forms.

As for the prevailing poetic forms in Soviet Latvian poetry today, one
is tempted to generalize, though with some caveats, that the evolution
of Latvian poetry both in Soviet Latvia and outside occurred almost
simultaneously. In the late fifties, not long after the "Hell's Kitchen" co-
terie and kindred spirits started to publish verse that signaled a depar-
ture from the canons of Latvian prosody, many Soviet Latvian poets
abandoned the strictures of traditional forms in preference for free
verse of various types, or "opened forms," a term of wide currency
among Soviet Latvian critics. As usual, the first iconoclasts were greeted
with some indignation, but soon the more sympathetic critics jumped
on the bandwagon with explanations that differ little from arguments
advanced in the West. The transfiguration of the formalistic aspects of
poetry, it is said, reflects the contemporary experience, which can no
longer subscribe to the notions of causality, chronology, and logical
structuration. A poem may very well be a record of consciousness, a free
flow of associations. The famous Archibald McLeish line, "a poem
should not mean / but be," has its repercussions even in Soviet Latvian
poetry. It is further argued that a poem that eschews the dramatic se-
quencing from exposition to denouement invites the reader to complete
it and to arrive at his or her own particular reading of it. Regularity,
clarity, and transparency are to be supplanted by complexity, opacity, a
certain hermetism. Many Soviet Latvian critics saw in the diversifica-
tion of poetic forms the distinct features of the sixties and seventies.[20]
But free verse, as some critics insist, never totally displaced traditional
versification, which in the seventies evidenced a significant resurgence.
Thus, the French or Italian sonnet is still popular with some contem-
porary poets. A shortened sonnet is another variant of the classical
form. The triolet is practiced with a great deal of success by Jānis Peters,
a poet of prominence in Soviet Latvia. A modified version of the tro-
chaic quatrains of *dainas* is also found with some poets. In short, the
range extends from classical verse forms to experiments with epis-

trophe of phonemic analogues as the compositional and semantic construct of a poem. Among the six poets in the present anthology, Olga Lisovska and Ārija Elksne gravitate toward traditional forms and toward a personal lyrical expression.

Ārija Elksne (b. 1928) is the author of several volumes of poetry and some critical studies. In one of her critical articles on contemporary poetry she complains that "sometimes form becomes so complicated that it obscures content. . . . And when the poem is finally deciphered, the reader uncovers nothing new." The poet certainly practices what she preaches. Critics have praised the precision, clarity, and unity of her verse, where form and content are tightly welded together, and emotion and intellect sustained in careful balance. The title poem of her collection, *Klusuma krastā* [On the Shores of Silence] sums up her poetic range: "I live on the shores of silence / Where flowers and children grow." Elksne invites the reader to celebrate the privileged moments of womanhood and motherhood. From these shores of silence arise flights into the past and future, and the woman/mother figure transforms into the symbol of the land. Survival on "that little strip of land visited by hatred and war" has been predicated on the fortitude of the Latvian woman, without whom "long ago the floods of war would have washed my people from earth." A sense of national historical destiny is very much in evidence in Elksne's poetry: "We are part of a spiral / Winding through generations / And little by little untwining / Thousands of strengths and capabilities."[21] Elksne has not escaped critical reprobation for her thematic preoccupations, incurring resentment for her "narrowness as a poetess of family idyll." Elksne shares some of these traits with Lisovska.

Olga Lisovska also has several volumes of poetry to her credit. Furthermore, she is known as a critic and editor of considerable achievement. Like Elksne, she abstains from heroic and epic subjects and couches her poetry in more traditional forms. If she occasionally indulges in some misanthropic contemplation of the contemporary scene, the tone is always muted, never inflated with the self-righteousness that is so often the point of view of the indignant moralist. Her reflections are modulated on a wide range of lyrical intonations, clearly articulated, and well balanced in their intellectual and emotional impact. Motifs from *dainas* are often interwoven into the texture of her verse, as if to underline the continuity of national values and experiences in the present. Thus, a well-known refrain, "Trīs priedītes siliņā" [three fir trees in a patch of woods], bewailing the ravages of war, suggests the ravages inflicted upon the people and the land by centuries of wars. Yet "the chain tying generation to generation / has not been broken."[22] Belševica's poetry is colored in darker tones.

Vizma Belševica is at the very forefront among Soviet Latvian poets. Suffering from poor health, she has been leading an existence of utter precariousness on the threshold of total debilitation and recovery. Similarly, her literary career has known setbacks and rehabilitation. Her books have been denounced and recalled. She was officially excommunicated and banned from publication during the years of imposed silence, and made a living through translations. Nevertheless, Belševica is steadily gaining in recognition outside her native land. Her poems have appeared in many anthologies in a number of languages, and three of her collections of poems have been published in Russian.

In addition to poetry, she has also published two collections of short stories. Her creative disposition is gravitating toward black humor that dwells on tragicomic eccentricities found in human relations, which are so deliberately warped as to elicit laughter and shuddering. The plots, fluctuating in plausibility, are all elaborated with a certain logic gone delirious. As if written during moments of repose from the travails of poetry, the stories are set in a light major clef that turns tragic and minor in her poetry.

In form, Belševica's poetry evidences little penchant for novelty, but there is a great variety of rhythms and tonal effects, sometimes difficult to be recreated in another language. The hallmark of her poetry is ontological introspection, a probe into the very depths of being. Hence, biblical and mythological figures are presented as archetypes that, as if imbedded in the collective unconscious transcending time and space, haunt the present. She frequently turns away from the ritualized banalities of contemporary urban life to the national past. In "The Notations of Henry the Latvian on the Margins of the Livonian Chronicle," Belševica evokes the suffering of the people, the lament of the conquered land that surges from the depth of the collective memory and casts its pall over the present and the future. Her poem "Night Indentations"[23] is another example of Belševica's opacity and density. On the most immediate level of meaning, the poem describes a nightmarish somnambulation through the streets of Riga, with sights both familiar and bizarre. The poem also suggests a retreat into the lost dreams of childhood, a plunge into that "alert infallibility of supraconsciousness" in search of a "connecting word"—perhaps Rimbaud's "verbe métaphysique"—that will unlock the secrets and marvels of being.

Belševica's poetry shares propensities with the poetry of her contemporaries in its thematic treatment of the conjunctures of the personal with the universally human, and the collective with the retrospectively prophetic. There are always intonations of poignancy and melancholy that mingle with a dogged faith in life—the "élan vital"—that enabled the Latvian to persevere through the darkest periods of his history. "Despair, / thy name is love's muteness in thy look! / . . . There will be other years . . . but the eyes of daisies will guide us on the autumnal roads of spite." Imants Ziedonis, another Soviet Latvian poet of Belševica's generation, in many ways is closely related to her.

Perhaps more than any other poet, Ziedonis basks in the intense glare of popularity as the national bard par excellence. His poetry extends over a wide scale of emotional tonalities and thematic preoccupations. As the critic Lija Brīdaka once suggested, "His personality is as original as the eye of the bee, endowed with the faculty for multiple vision."[24] This multiple vision registers impressions from the contemporary world, as well as from the past and the potential. Ziedonis's themes are a reflection of a personality that can be impulsive and nervous, waxing impatient and angry, a personality subject to onslaughts of lassitude and melancholy, bursting out alternately in morose irony and joyful affirmation of life.

The range of Ziedonis's work comprises short, witty bagatelles playing with sounds and rhythms, and poetic prose pieces with epic sweeps of philosophic profundity. "Let me be myself," is the *cri de coeur* of Ziedonis, inveighing against all those—bureaucrats, technocrats, bigots, and their retinue—who encroach upon his personal freedom and promote the ugly and the impure. In his *Epifānijas* [Epiphanies], Ziedonis celebrates those privileged moments, experienced daily in the course of routine encounters with humans, animals, and things, when life, under whatever form it may be, bursts forth in its beauty, clarity, and innocence. These are moments of heightened consciousness of living in depth, consciousness of reaching into the very heart of being and distilling truth and the joy of life. *Kurzemíte* [Courland] is a series of meditative travelogues recording the poet's impressions from the old province of Latvia. It is a probe into the Latvian psyche, its contradictions and aspirations, as well as an assessment of the devastation that modern social and economic progress leaves in its wake. Natural beauty is obliterated, traces of the national past are erased, and crass materialism is seducing the people as everything becomes geared to greater efficiency and productivity. And the poet wonders if the eggs of the little bird will be more precious to the child than the fake diamonds.[25]

Though there are moments of misanthropy and of temptation to withdraw into oneself and let the world be as it is, a deep sense of responsibility subtends Ziedonis's poetry. The moral imperative makes the poet feel guilty and indignant about the world around him, the degradation of values and the dangers of materialism. The poet is also the curator of the Latvian language. For Ziedonis that means not only celebration of its beauties and exploration of its unknown riches, but also the responsibility to preserve the language uncontaminated by the banalities of consumer society and to impart a sense of preciousness to his reader, who may not recognize the language's precariousness. In many ways, Ziedonis, who is so much quoted and adulated, can claim to be the conscience of the people.

Among the first generation of Soviet Latvian poets that appeared on the literary scene after World War II, Māris Čaklais is the youngest (b. 1940). His work, however, has attained considerable proportions in volume as well as in quality. Besides being the author of some nine collections of poetry, Čaklais is also accredited as a respectable essayist and translator. Critics are wont to call him the poet of youth. Being the youngest among his peers, he apparently has great appeal to those who refuse to be counted among the adults. And if youth is changing moods, restlessness, a vision of an ideal that scorns the actual and the up-to-date, Čaklais can very well pass for the ombudsman of the generation that follows his. Other critics have noted his affinities with Bertolt Brecht, whose works he has been translating into Latvian. Čaklais poems are frequently characterized by informality and conversational directness, and are well suited, as discovered by a number of Soviet Latvian composers, for light entertainment performances. But this is not to say that his poetry is lightweight.

Čaklais's poetry is intensely personal, and its tonal range is wide. In rapid succession the emotional register can change from joy to grief, invoking inner harmonies and schizophrenic self-search. Doubt and derision supplant affirmation and responsiveness, and rarely do "the torturous whys fall silent." But generally Čaklais's shadings are nocturnal, his tones elegiac and rural. Man's need to be close to nature is best articulated through the contrasts of urban frenzy and rural harmonies. Living in rhythms synchronic with the life cycles of nature, the Latvian country folk are depicted as paragons of sanity, frugality, and contentment derived from hard work. Čaklais's landscape, colored in with serene arcadian hues, clashes with the scenes from the "Feast of the Fat and the Opulent."

The contemporary urban scene, epitomized by the traffic jam, "crowded streets, air, motor to motor, fright to fright, sorrow to sorrow," is banal and repulsive. Inevitably the poet's vision turns often to the past. The old inner city of Riga still guards remnants of the glories and beauty of the old Hanseatic town; it tempts the poet, with its permanence and its challenge to the present, to become part of it, a paving stone, a root of the old elm tree. The past and the present seem to be irreconcilably opposed. A fragment of *dainas* is ironically contrasted with the jingle of the contemporaries, pointing out the hollowness of the present. It seems that the poet, too, being a witness of his times, must accept the notion that poetry, at first, necessitates an experience of loss. Čaklais asks: "Has that much been taken away from you that you can be a poet?" There is, however, a possibility of redemption and fulfillment. The poet must reassert his ties with the people. After a poetry day in a country town, the poet proclaims his *raison d'être*: "How good to feel the burden. You're still here and we are still."

If Čaklais can be characterized as the poet of youth, intensely personal, straightforward, and sincere, his recently deceased contemporary Ojārs Vācietis (1933–83) is often referred to, for better or for worse, as the Latvian Yevtushenko. The sobriquet is not gratuitous. His earlier works—he published a dozen poetry collections—are paeans of sorts to the order of things as they are. His later productions, however, become philosophical and probing at times, as well as openly critical, pleading for a socialism with a more human face. On occasion he quite courageously engaged some of the hard core dogmatists and sycophants in battles over the mission of the arts and literature. Popular as a poet, essayist, and orator, Vācietis passed for the spokesman of the new generation of the sixties, calling for the repudiation of the Stalin era and rededication to the rights of the individual. Interspersing his accusations of the establishment with an occasional homage to the greatness of Lenin or the glories of the Red Banner, Vācietis, like Yevtushenko, was tolerated as an acceptable dissident whose presence demonstrates to the outside world that freedom of speech does indeed exist in the Soviet Union. The balancing act, of course, was fraught with dangers, but it was surely challenging and stimulated ingenuity. "Manuscripts do not burn," Vācietis declared with audacity and impunity.

Critics are generous with their praise of Vācietis's talent, calling him an innovative poet with insights susceptible of unveiling new facets of reality. At times his poetry reaches for epic grandeur and universality of meaning, and there transpire the Protean moods of his complex personality, a personality that may appear sophisticated and at times blunt, elegiac and sarcastic, soaring with *joie de vivre* and weighed down by weariness of life. History is a nightmare from which there is no awakening, to paraphrase Joyce. "There are narrow old streets, / capillaries, / where the blood of history, / rosy, alive and / tangibly human, / comes coursing into your fingers / which hurry has numbed, / and restores / their sensitive touch."[26] The past is likely to evoke an apocalyptic vision of the future, since man has heeded little the lessons of history and seems to be heading, given his fascination with war and with atomic bombs, toward a world inhabitable by primitive creatures, reptiles, and insects. If Vācietis's intransigence and misanthropy vary with his moods, his visceral need for arcadian simplicities is unchanging. With Vācietis, nature's bio-rhythms seem to be translated into poetic rhythms. "We extend into the totality before us and into the totality that comes after us."

By Way of Conclusion

Shifting perhaps the intended meaning of the Vācietis line quoted above, we can readily see sequences of generations—predecessors, contemporaries, successors of kindred spirits. Besides Elksne, Lisovska, Belševica, Ziedonis, and Čaklais, there are many other names in Soviet Latvian poetry that merit mention. Imants Auziņš, Jānis Peters, and Uldis Zariņš are poets greatly respected for their poetic achievement, personal courage and sense of responsibility toward the people. Some Soviet Latvian poets have been severely censored by critics and guardians of ideological purity. Others have suffered outright banishment and imprisonment. One should not, however, infer from these observations that Soviet Latvian poetry has as its dominant trait some kind of expression of anti-socialist dissent. In most instances, the dissent proceeds from a sense of injustice and alarm, from the recognition of misuses and abuses of human beings and national resources by a system that was supposed to give back dignity to all human beings. This stance is perhaps even more visible among the younger generation of poets, "the totality that comes after us," to cite Vācietis's line. Jānis Rokpelnis, Bērziņš, Juris Helds, and other poets of their generation (born in the late forties) are often bent on aggressive satire, trenchant parody, mordant wit. And yet next to the indictment of the senselessness of modern society, there are nostalgic tones and affirmation of the ultimate values of human life.

And, to pursue the Vācietis quotation, "we extend into the totality before us," it is not difficult to see affinities in this volume between the Soviet Latvian poets and the poets outside Latvia, who are generally older by several years. In both cases, the poet's conscious response and his impulse are similar in their search for authentic values and identity through the cultivation of the most precious possession: the Latvian language. There is, of course, a marked distinction between the two groups. As Joseph Brodsky contends, writers in repressive societies are forced to take words more seriously than writers who have the luxury of saying anything. Hence, Soviet Latvian poetry is not afflicted in the same way with the disease that Roland Barthes diagnosed in our petit bourgeois culture as semantic obesity of words, a disease in which words are overfed with meaning. On the other side of the ideological divide, Barthe's interpretation of the Orpheus myth acquires new significations. There, literature cuts like a two-edged sword. According to Barthes, literature is expected to ask the most important questions that beset man. Yet literature is not to provide answers, not to ask questions in such a way that the answer is already implied in the question. Orpheus (i.e. literature) is to lead Eurydice out of Hades to the light of meaning. But as soon as he turns around to look at his beloved, and thereby names meaning, he kills Eurydice, since named meaning is dead meaning. Named meaning may be dead, but it may also mean dead Orpheus, literally and figuratively. Naming meaning may be dangerous to one's physical health, and Orpheus may also die for not having named meaning for those who need spiritual sustenance and guidance.

The poet outside Latvia, however, does not carry that weight of responsibility, since solidarity and compassion for the complacent survivor in exile, which has long ceased to be exile, are gratuitous. But apart from the differences that may proceed from the geopolitical situation of the poet, both groups of poets share the trauma and nostalgia of the past, and both groups share the anxieties and the aspirations with which Latvians view their national destiny in the years to come. But Latvian poetry is more than preoccupation with what is Latvian. It speaks to the world, to people everywhere. Pasternak is reported to have said that Latvian poets have remained where poetry itself still lives: close to the grass.

Notes

1 Czeslaw Milosz, *Native Realm*, tr. C. S. Leach (Garden City, N.Y.: Doubleday & Co. 1968), p. 7.

2 See "Interview with Czeslaw Milosz," *Association for the Advancement of Baltic Studies Newsletter* 6 (April 1982).

3 Alfreds Bilmanis, *A History of Latvia* (Princeton: Princeton University Press, 1951), p. 21.

4 See William R. Schmalstieg, "The Lithuanian Language—Past and Present," *Lituanus* 28:5-26, from which the present discussion is derived.

5 These observations are taken from an unpublished article, "The Latvian Language," by Valdis Zeps.

6 See "On the Threat of Linguistic Assimilation" *Lituanus* 23:56.

7 An English version was published in *The New York Times*, Feb. 27, 1972.

8 *Amberland* 41 (1980):6.

9 *AABS Newsletter* 6 (April 1982):5.

10 Quoted in Jānis Rudzītis, *Starp Provinci and Eiropu* (Västeras Ziemeļblāzma, 1971), p. 13. Translation mine.

11 See Valdis Zeps, "Folk Meter and Latvian Verse," *Lituanus* 19:10-26.

12 See Vaira Vīķis-Freibergs, "Echoes of the *Dainas* and the Search for Identity in Contemporary Latvian Poetry," *Journal of Baltic Studies* 6:17–29.

13 Yves Bonnefoy, "On the Translation of Form in Poetry," *World Literature Today* 52 (Summer 1979):375–76.

14 Baiba Bičole, *Griežos* (New York: Grāmatu Draugs, 1981), p. 27.

15 Professor Rolfs Ekmanis, in his massive study, *Latvian Literature under the Soviets* (Belmont, Mass.: Nordland Publishing Co., 1978), distinguishes four phases in the postwar period: 1) Zhdanov repression, 1946–1953; 2) Khrushchev thaw, 1953–1957; 3) Backlash, 1957–1960; 4) Struggle for cultural survival, 1960 to present.

16 See George Lukacs, *Histoire de la conscience de classe* (Paris: Editions de Minuit, 1960).

17 Pierre Henri Simon, *L'Esprit et l'histoire* (Paris: Colin, 1954), pp. 14–15. Translation mine.

18 See Valda Melngaile, "The Sense of History in Recent Soviet Latvian Poetry," *Journal of Baltic Studies* 6:130–40.

19 Wilson Harris, *History, Fable and Myth* (Georgetown, Guyana, 1970), p. 21.

20 See articles by M. Kalve and V. Ķikāns in *Žanrs un Kanons* (Riga: Zinātne, 1977).

21 Ārija Elksne, *Treša Bezgalība* (Riga: Liesma, 1971), p. 31. Translation by Valda Melngaile.

22 Olga Lisovska, *Pie Jūsu Mīlestības* (Riga: Liesma, 1973), p. 106.

23 The translator, faced with many options, chose this particular title, which is ripe with associations in English. Yet it does not quite match the multiple meanings of the Latvian word "atkāpes," which can also signify "retreat," "concessions," "withdrawal."

24 Lija Brīdaka, *Kritikas Gada Grāmata* (Riga: Liesma, 1973), p. 234. Translation mine.

25 Imants Ziedonis, *Kurzemīte* (Riga: Liesma, 1974), p. 61. Translation mine.

26 Ojārs Vācietis, "History," *Amberland* 41 (1981):2.

THE TRANSLATORS

Inara Cedrins
Astrīde Ivaska
Ivar Ivask
Juris Rozītis
Laris Saliņš
Ilze Šķipsna
Velta Sniķere
Ruth Speirs
Astrīda Stahnke
Bitīte Vinklers
and in a few cases
the poets themselves

EXILE LATVIAN POETS

LINARDS TAUNS   1922–1963

Linards Tauns (pseudonym of Arnolds Bērzs) left Latvia in 1944 to escape the Soviet occupation. He lived in various DP camps in Germany, before emigrating to the United States in 1950. Tauns settled in New York City and became a major figure in the "Hell's Kitchen" group. He worked as a typesetter and edited a Latvian journal. Modern French painting and ancient Egyptian, Etruscan, and Greek art, as well as the poetry of Baudelaire, Lorca, Apollinaire, and Dylan Thomas were studies which interested him. Tauns published one collection of verse before his early death. A posthumous book of poetry was edited by his close friend Gunārs Saliņš.

A FUNERAL TAKES PLACE IN THE CITY

A funeral takes place in the city
A prostitute's burial

The procession halts at important landmarks
                of her short-lived career
Steeped in the blinding light of her crazed eyes
It also halts in front of the restaurant
Where I saw her that day
And which now quite suddenly smells of carrion flies
Their color a romantic blue

They flutter their wings to agitate little flags
In honour of this solemn occasion

That day she waved some victorious or vanquished
                              nation's miniature flag
Because she had just been discharged
From the asylum

Upon her entrance
The restaurant filled with unbearable noise
There screamed from her the whole past
Not only her own but the past of us all
Screamed
Trombone-accompanied
With such intensity
As if this woman
Were the old Russian emigree
Who had fled abroad with the Tsar
Shot in the cellar of Yekaterinburg

She entered
And her unmasking presence
Made every face transparent
I saw through each
The table at the back and its coffee cups
Filled like vases with neatly trimmed
                              meadow and garden flowers
But her own face
Was like blossoms crushed between a book's pages
They still emitted some scent
Before they each spread their arms
Along an indiscernable crucifix
As if nailed to the Cross

Flowers indeed were her attribute
Her lovers blossom as poppies in Flanders
Fifteen years since the Second World War

Fear constantly raged in her eyes
Not like our fear of cats' yellow faces

Nor of a broken mirror
Nor the new moon across the left shoulder
But fear
Of the perdition of chastity

She approached me suddenly saying
Mister I am a virgin
And I'll die as such

And she died as such

A funeral takes place in the city

Ruth Speirs

DREAM OF A TOWN

I want to make sure that my town is indeed
As it appears in my dreams.
Therefore, taking my dream, I shall go
Where Vincent gathered the sun and teashops and wheat,
I shall place my dream on vistas of fruit trees,
On fruit, on two furtively peering
Small boys with trousers at half-mast,
On wooden fences, on scatter brained dogs,
On lilies-of-the-valley scattered in gardens—
Against all these, I shall measure my dream
To make sure it is true.
Looking at lopsided roofs, I shall think: How good
                              that my dream is lopsided too,
And it must not, must not ever be wrong.
Two children peering at clouds reflected in puddles,
                              their trousers at half-mast,
Will admit me into the town, accepting my dream
                              as a passport,
And the password will be: The Perpetual Cloud.

And I entered the town, and I placed my dream
                              on its stones,

And saw: they were older even than my remotest
                         past lives, long gone.
Pharoahs sleep in them, clasped by the Sun.
The town dreams *us*. We don't dream the town.

   Ruth Speirs

FEASTING

And then we were asked to a feast
where we wondered—
is it our beloved that we touch,
or are we holding
earthen vessels between our hands?

Aglow with pale radiance, they were given to us,
and we held in them through a distant light
fields of wheat
and faces in flower,
but when we clinked them,
voices rang out, singing
at a vintage feast of very long ago.

The hostess of this house—
three graces in aquatint.
Time and space were
but a song
when the lines
of the two draped bodies and one bared
played for us
noble yet intimate music.

As one unearths ancient temples,
we unearthed smiles on faces
that had been sleeping in lips and eyes

as in Pompeii
for two thousand years.

Yet we could not uncover
the veil of two eyes.

Astrīde Ivaska

THE OLD HOUSE

Returning,
Old house, I hear: a fruit in your garden falls with a thud,
Falls, intertwined with the sun,
Thuds, intertwining with marigolds, dahlias and larkspur.
Beneficence streams from you to the world
      undeflected, in luminous furrows:
You have abundance of love.
We strain to support the back-breaking weight of remembrance,
But you, old house, you hold the bygone old world
On your shoulder, as light as a bird.

Before we vanish, we try to discern
      the trumpet call of our future.
You say: You will hear it all from the bird
      that sits on my shoulder, cooing.

With all my strength I cling to your warm wooden doorposts
That I, a city's sleepwalker, might not see
      —on iron-work, towers and bridges—
The far-away heralds' chilling blue glitter
Before the tentative dawn of my day.

Ruth Speirs

A DOG IS LYING BY THE CITY GATES

A dog is lying by the city gates,
Prostrate,
As though he'd been there for centuries gone,
As though, a young soldier, he fell
    defending the city this early dawn.

The dog is alive, and no Cerberus
Who casts his shadow across the city,
Whose barking rasps in our throat, in our chest
And shatters the windows in every street.
As though we were blind, he ushers us into the city,
    taking the lead.

He looks at its beautiful women
And seems very old and wise
As though he had seen them fighting
    on rubble and barricades,
As though he stuck out his tongue
          as he eyes
The buildings nobly erected since then.
But where windows recite
Poems, he listens inspired.

He might be my playmate and childhood companion,
The dog I remember well from our outings.
With the merciless yell of warriors storming a citadel,
Across sandpits, communal swimming pools, merry-go-rounds,
He howled
As I bawled:
"Surrender, world!"
But longest of all we strolled
    through puddles in dreamy meditation
As girls in gardens
    walk among beds of carnations.

He leads us into the city as though we were blind,
For scents and sounds to fall around our necks
    and embrace us.

Like ourselves, he has scars of every kind,
But the dog is a poet all right:
Where roofs are constructed like stanzas
He laughs with enlightened delight.
Why do we need a dog as we enter the city?
Because our wailing has ceased.
Because our despairing howls at the moon are finished.
The world has gone drunk. Lick its face!

Do you think that a guide will lead us to Paradise?
No!—the dog for the blind,
A silken strand in the thread through the labyrinth.

  Ruth Speirs

VAN GOGH'S POTATO EATERS

With wild shouts, we walk,
we are
horns tooting on highways
along which we escape our own selves,
saxophones among saxophones,
nurslings avid for she-wolf's milk.

At us, silence shouts.
Neither smoke in coffee houses, where faces inseparably merge,
nor summer's transparency, where even quivering air is visible,
can give us clarity, can give us nebulae,
for they are, one and all,
a stunning blow that falls
straight on our foreheads.

In silence, like the Thief at night,
there enters one life unlived, millions of lives lost,
words that did not turn into kisses,
soulless souls,
a cruel century, Christ for the second time,

echoing footfalls fleeing across bridges broken in two.
Therefore we denude our nights of silence,
suddenly stumbling in empty rooms
over torn veils.
It is stumbling that we cross this threshold.

Colors rush at us,
colors of fruit and of streets.
We expected a sacred procession whirling
across our canvases,
nuns from the Convent of the Sacred Heart
in gaudily worldly dress,
but this is an attack,
a march against us in closed formations,
bayonets dripping with the blood of fruit and of streets.
Tell us, fusiliers, where should we dip our brushes?
—Into your masks, reflected in puddles of wine.

We walk
with majorettes,
with minarets,
with wild shouts for she-wolf's milk.
Suddenly, in Brabant, the procession stops.
We are seated
around the table of Van Gogh's Potato Eaters.

Astrīde Ivaska

ONCE, UPON ENTERING GARDENS

Once, upon entering gardens,
I remembered
How deep I had drunk of their wines—
And my songs in their praise, most of all
On their aspect of dying blossoms
Resurrected in fruit.
And the gardens surmised I had come

10   Linards Tauns

On a great and festive occasion.
They welcomed me, kissing my cheek
And, unfurling their flags,
Filed past me as though on parade
While I stood underneath
Ever new
Ever changeable
Breezes scattering pollen.
And then they unveiled my memorial,
Suddenly dipping their flags.

Ruth Speirs

THE TEASHOP

And crossing the bridges, I found
Peace there, and small
Inconspicuous streets,
And surrounded by freckled
     cheerfully clamoring children
I entered the yellow
Teashop where plants climbed through windows
Into the room.

Where time had been brought to a halt
And tasted of wholesome cheese
Because the small street
Was full of the meadows' great peace.

And things were as gentle as sisters.
I merged with them all
And became the yellow
Paint on the teashop's walls

And the poetry of the small street
And a child's voice, cheerfully raised,

And a speck, a freckle
On the tearoom's face.

I drank orangeade there,
Aware
First of one, then another, and then of them all—
About fifteen smells on the little boys' hands
Which had fingered, fondled and whacked
And blended with
Hundreds of things:

Nail lacquer, grease, the insides of clocks,
        the ribbons in little girls' plaits,
Valerian, the tail of a cat,
The green out-of-doors, the whiteness of sheets,
        and flower pots, and the wind,
And big sister's lipsticks, and milk,
Cobblestones, steam, and rust . . .

Boys and hundreds of scents, all fusing,
Rushed like bees from a hive, humming and buzzing—
In the sheerest blue round the bridges I crossed
The summer's honeycomb dripped slow drops.

Ruth Speirs

STEPPING OUT IN THESE STREETS

Stepping out in these streets
Is like drifting away in the rivers' sweep.

In a shop window, pots of paint on display,
But my glance strays past them to former days:
Tarred old roofs, and fences painted a long time ago,
And I with paint-stained hands, and tar on my toes,
Roamed as I pleased
        with blissful contentment and ease

In a world that was apple-green.
My uncle in the Salvation Army
Pounded his drums at every rally;
I smeared them all over with paint,
And when he set out to proclaim
        the end of the world, he looked pained
Since the world and its mischiefs are ever reborn.
But *I* meant no harm—
In a world that was green
I was green and speckled and happy as happy can be,
All the colors blended and fused into light for me.

Stepping out in these streets
Is like drifting away in the rivers' sweep . . .

   Ruth Speirs

THE ARTIST'S STUDIO

Does he live
Here
In this place
Where his brush strokes,
A smile on canvas,
Slip between lips and eyes into space?

Other brush strokes
Enter
From landscapes, from breasts, and snows.
Other
Brush strokes enter
From exclamations at meeting, from the monotonous
Sing-song of rivers, from sorrow, sorrow at railway stations,
From pale
Wine glasses, filled or drained dry,

Brush strokes
Enter his pale fevered face.

The pallor of fever
In lips and eyes—
As if the morning,
He dawns over glasses of wine.

Ah,
The fever contained in the eyes of the morning—
Drained lips and eyes:
Pale glasses of wine.

Whether he lives in this place,
Here, among landscapes with snows,
Among nudes with breasts like the snow,
Or whether this place
Space, lives within him—
Its snows burn within him—
No one can tell.

   Ruth Speirs

THE WASHERWOMAN

Three puddles mirror
wash hanging on a line,
as if with reflections
a master were painting,
"Washday."

Between pieces of clothing, the washerwoman's smile
looks out of the painting, windblown,

scrubbed for many days, dried for many days,
faded now, like all those days.

A cloud hangs among lace curtains,
tablecloths, towels,
the blue of the sky drips from its folds.

Reflection,
I shall take you and make
of you and the blue of the sky
a delicate handkerchief
for the washerwoman.

Astrīde Ivaska

ALL SOULS' DAY

All Souls' Day,
day when all is one,
fish, stars and stone,
day when the fragrance of the world
is that of flowers on graves
and in the hands of young girls.

On this day gentle girls brought me flowers
as if it were my birthday.
But how could I have been born on All Souls' Day?
They should rather have taken
one green leaf and placed it
on my future grave.

Yet they brought me flowers.
Huge red gladioli on tall stems
swayed in my senses

like bloodstained, tattered regimental flags,
barricades raised high,

fragments of old films, showing duels and wars.
From these huge red flowers waved to me
redhaired women in loosened garments
who once set Jerusalem aflame.
I knew then: the girls want their gardens
to winter in my breath.
Yet their fragile hands and their armpits
hide a dreadful weapon—dead years and centuries long dead.

But someone said, "I know,
I know where your eyes are now,
since your beloved died—
they bloom as gladioli among graveyard grass.
But do not, do not look at flowers
as if they were dust.
For all is one,
fish, stars and stone—
and you shall love today
the shapes that stand between flowers and eyes,
between lips and clay."

Astrīde Ivaska

IN SEARCH OF A SONG

Scanning the streets
in search of a song,
I look at the maze
of the world so immense,
charmed and dazed,
I turn my ear,
hear-
ing the sounds of the world—
no, with every sense

for this world I grope in haste—
I touch it, I fill up my lungs,
I drink it, I taste
the world on my tongue,
in search of a song.

Astrīde Ivaska

ASTRĪDE IVASKA   1926–

Astrīde Ivaska left Latvia in 1944. She studied classical and modern languages at the University of Marburg in Germany. With her husband, the Estonian poet and critic Ivar Ivask, she emigrated to the United States in 1949 and settled first in Minnesota. Since 1967 she has been living in Norman, Oklahoma, where Ivar Ivask edits the international literary quarterly, World Literature Today. *Astrīde Ivaska has published four volumes of poetry since 1966, a collection of prose sketches, and a children's book, for which she received, among others, the Zinaida Lazda Prize and Culture Foundation of Latvians Prize for Literature.*

TABLE AFTER SUPPER

The spokes of hollowed-out grapefruit, pinkish, sticky moist,
whirl like the sun's chariot in the candles' flickering circle.
Trickles of molten wax; scattered salt bodes evil;
the charred potato skin—a tired, flattened moth.

The table's work accomplished, it retires into itself.
Apples roll inward to their cores, the tablecloth recalls the
    rettery.
In glasses awakens the tiny laughter of sandgrains;
in the candles, honeycombs rustle; in the dishes, river reeds
    whisper.
From the candlestick's forked branches rolls down a drop of
    wax,

an amber-yellow drop.
Light years and dark years, voices of birds and the sea
call out against the wind.

  Ivar Ivask

IN VIENNA'S FORESTS

There it appears again, the white boat of the wind. Between
tall silvery beech trees it slides along Vienna's forest valley, light
as a ray of brilliance. Three mighty sails, tall and full-blown by a
wind felt only by us both. I watch it slip into the tree trunks'
shadowy silver, haze veiling the seam it leaves behind.

A grey trunk closes the road to us. Early fall storm. Roots hold
the wheel of earth in a tight grasp, cling to it still while in air.
Too high to step over. Palms sticky with yellowish, gravelly
earth. It's always damp in these wrinkles of earth, in these over-
grown ravines. But we don't linger, only slip through like a boat
in the wind of the heart. Nothing holds us. We are begun, but
will remain unfinished. Only one moment, retained in a yellow-
ing photograph, from some windy day in a time past.

  Inara Cedrins

SWANS

The ship slides into Cobh harbor: frost on the hillsides,
they shimmer grey-green like tarnished silver. Houses
in pastel colors—rosy, bluish, greenish, golden. A covey
of black pochard ducks flutters up from the water. An island
of dark towers, stone ruins, cypresses ruffled by the wind.
Not at all like a nature scene—rather part of a painting
seen in childhood in some twilit room. All is ordered in a rhythm
and pattern familiar to the eye, seen long ago and then

forgotten. Swans too. Swans? Of course, this painting needs
swans in shadowy water. There they appear, and I
don't even wonder at them. Land of black pochards. Forest
swan land. Land of recalled rhythm. Gentle, veiled, feminine land.
Water-cradled land of bounded shores. Land, land,
land. Hoar-frosted memory-glazed land.

   Inara Cedrins

ZINNIAS AND SMOKED FISH

The room smelled of zinnias and smoked fish,
the balcony swam in the tree tops,
oak leaves splintered the day.
O Saint Sebastian, you are shot full of summer's arrows!
When happy you die, your body glitters of light.
Deep below sparkled the water's tautly-drawn sail;
it caught us, warm and tough, with seams of sparks,
when we fled towards the shore which, dusky and steep,
entwined us in shadows of weeds and sagging branches.

Shadows are brittle and weightless, yet light is heavy.
Water gives strength to endure it, so do the trees,
the smoked fish and the moon's empty plate.

   Ivar Ivask

ON THE ISLAND OF PAROS

It would be good to spend one's life on Paros,
where old people die looking out at the sea,
leaving steep little streets and fig trees behind,
shadowy doorways with rocking chairs and cats,
the Hundred-Pillar Church against the steps of flat hills,

and the forgotten god in the quarry
who has to sleep so far from the sea.

Ivar Ivask

SEPTEMBER IN SCOTLAND

Cattle move dark in the pasture.
The quicksets have chopped up the sun,
scattered its radiance, letting
it swill the animals' feet.

A bull with rosy horns—
the evening is stalking the heath,
where only bees were permitted
to tread in yellow boots.

The eyes of the mountains mist over.
The pattern of quickset grows faint.
Within hives the summer thickens
to humming honeycomb darkness.

Ivar Ivask

K.H.

You were the first to leave
of our summer friends.
Between your house and the granary
are still woodlands—
slender birches and the junipers'
bristly fur coats
against fresh pine growth,
tight in the darkness.
Strawberry beds relax under the snow,
the hawk that was hung up as scarecrow

stiffens. Life has lifted off on waxen wings.
The lathe drowses in the granary,
unused blocks of birch wood
feel about with their blind eyes.
On this island frozen in snow, twilight settles.
Each day at this hour
on the sills, cabinets, shelves,
the cranes
stretch out their necks and softly
begin calling in the silence.

Inara Cedrins

I AWAKEN

I awaken in your world's warmly cupped hands
        and all is well.
The gates of the forest are still closed,
but in the distance already drones
        my postponed life.
Peewits clamor and magpies laugh:
                        guard
your jewels and heart!
        The lake smiles
with mischievous eyes, awakening the waterlilies.
This morning the sharp point of pain is broken.
        To leave and to turn back are one
                in your quiet world.

Inara Cedrins

FRAILTY

Frailty,
tilled earth,
a sowing awaiting possibilities.
You must nurse yourself along,
you've been seeded,
there by the reddened stubble,
beside the hawthorn bush.

Bitter hawthorn breath,
frailty,
tenacious roots.
A strange fear by day,
and nightly, harsh peace.

Inara Cedrins

From SEAWORDS

our room floats
on the sea's rippling,
crosses of light
and love.
Flying fish carry it far
into the open sea—
a tiny shimmering shell
permeated by deathlessness.

At that moment, when the stars stop
and you cross the threshold
of the dark counter-force,
through your blood will flash the lightning
of all the sea's dolphin dance

Inara Cedrins

Astrīde Ivaska   23

RETURNING TO ROSS, CALIFORNIA

I would like to find a pen
belonging to the owner of this room
to write it all down:
the smell of well-scrubbed oak floors
and memories stored in lace-trimmed
pincushions.

Everything falls back into place.

We started out together.
We liked the same things,
we were friends
in a country no longer ours.

This is your daughter's room.
The first day of the year
fades behind white eyelet curtains.

I set under the stiff gaze
of a little girl,
painted ages ago—she must have
been here when you came—
a serious small girl in pigtails,
apricot brocade dress and velvet vest,
lace-bordered all around.
A green cockateel perched on one wrist,
in the other hand a pink.
A little girl in her world,
facing life squarely, about to
take the first step, wide-eyed,
unafraid.

It is so quiet here: an inner stillness
of years ago. Even the wild bees
are silent. Such a pity
to sell the house, you said—

the whole wall of Siri's room
is full of bees and honey.

The prim little girl
returns my gaze.
Behind the eyelet curtains
time flows slower
over lemon leaves.

   (*Originally written in English*)

SPRING, OKLAHOMA

Our movements those of a dazed awakening snake,
we weave cautiously around rains and rivers,
touching tasselled oaks, tufted pecans,
acorn-coned sumak, willows breathed in green,
redbuds retreating into the house of summer.
Slowly chewing the reddish flesh
around sinews of gullies,
tousling the wind-angled towheads of cedars,
we circle a low-branching land
under a pebbly, hawk-strewn sky.

   (*Orginally written in English*)

THE RAIN AND I

The rain and I
are sharing my house this morning—
the rain talks to me from outside,
and I answer back in turn.
The rain asks me this morning
about a wreath of white roses I made long ago.
Why did you not let me touch it,

says the rain, if it was all that beautiful?
I wanted to, but they shut it away from me.
Over her heart they laid my white rose wreath
when they took her away from me.
And they gave it to Fire.
And Fire took it away before you let me touch it,
says the rain. Forgive me, I say. But the rain
does not answer. And we both
fall silent this morning in my house,
the rain and I.

Inara Cedrins

ANCESTORS

There never was such a place,
there never were such people
except within you,
except in your memory.
And yet—touch this—
it is clay,
and this here—
it is amber.
They left it behind,
people who never were,
to remind you
of their passing.

Inara Cedrins

NEWS FROM THE SEA

1

On a misty morning I comb my hair in the garden,
facing a window that mirrors the sea. Yes—I remember what
   you told me,
Grandmother—I know I shouldn't. But I won't be here,
come Spring. And even if a bird should wind my
hair into its nest, if I'm far away, it won't give me
a headache . . . I am reflected in the wide window.
In it gleams the sea and Ringabella promontory
as it once will be mirrored by memory. Farther inside,
a glass door exposes me, combing my hair in the garden
this misty morning.

2

The spruce hedge limiting the pasture to the South throws
a midday shadow. It slashes off the tip of Ringabella sharply.
There are two hedges now—one stiff and straight,
the other spread over the ground, joined at a straight angle.
They are the same length exactly. Toward evening, the shadow
   hedge
will lengthen, or be wiped away by a squall of rain.

3

A flock of seagulls flits across Ringabella promontory. Against
greenish pasture, yellowed stubble, brown-green hedges,
they flutter like a handful of petals, visible one moment
and invisible the next, when they tilt their wings at right angles
to us. That is all that happened this late December afternoon:
the playful circles of gulls around Ringabella. But I was here
to see.

4

At full moon, flooding is sudden and sly, ebb slow-paced
and long. It leaves behind wide banks of sand
for gulls to hunt on and for people to ride horses
or walk about. It leaves seaweed and pebbles with news

Astrīde Ivaska   27

from the sea. They should be received in silence and solitude.
They are ancient, come from afar, and their message
is always the same. Everyone must decipher for himself
and hide them in the most secret place of the heart.
But however much one wishes, one cannot send
an answer back to the sea.

5

A ring of cold steel surrounds the full moon, and a white thread
has been pulled through the three stars of Orion's Belt. Ebb
by night, and the calls of strange birds. Are they hunting
on the sandbanks, or are they migratory birds flying
by night? The sea draws its heavy breath in the bay.

6

The West Wind always comes like a mailman by night
and rattles the letterbox till dawn, trying
to deliver a message entrusted to him alone. But it is not in
    writing
and he always has to move on, the task unaccomplished—
yet to return another time, and try again.

Inara Cedrins

TIDE

At about three in the afternoon the waters flood up. It is win-
ter, and the sun is on the very bottom step of the year; it is the
time of the greatest ebb of light. After the Winter Solstice the
light will flood in and around Easter-time will billow in floods of
light.

In Ringabella's bay there's a strong withdrawal today. It has
disclosed a rounded bank in the center of the bay—a shallow

shell. Over it ride three horsemen, two on dun horses, one on a roan, circled by three dogs.

Sensing the approach of water, seabirds begin calling, crows and gulls in roving flight. The pallor of sand is mottled with white and black spots. There are no people now: in the shallows float forest swans. A strange tremor overtakes the sea.

And then the water returns. In smooth waves it slides toward the shallows, completely soundless, shortening the distance with each foaming step. The birds draw together and run toward the middle, but don't leave the bank. No—yet others flutter down, as though something important were happening here, some ancient changeless celebration: the slow stepping back of earth before sea, water and earth flowing into one. The opposite of what happened when God divided solid earth from water in order to create a world. Returning tide destroys the world of birds created by ebb. Without pause it climbs, drawing a curve around the bank. The sea has already flooded into the lower depressions and cut off the point of the bank. All occurs in silence—from time to time only the disturbed laughter of a gull echoes.

The floods come in a different manner than waves breaking against the shore. These swaths draw near as though from the furthest distance, not running and not stepping back. They flow in, not able to be stopped and silent, taking that which is theirs without pausing until all is taken. Around and past the shoal they come, vanishing beyond the promontory's distant end. Neither are they divided in flailings as are the sea's squalls against the promontory, as sentences and words uttered by the sea. In waves of tide the sea sings. They rise and fall in a song's undivided flow.

As the shoal grows smaller, the green depth of water at the opposite shore grows deeper. The tighter the curve of water is drawn, the more calm and quiet the birds become. And then suddenly the shore's cedars are filled with wild doves: the flood's veil covers the bank. The waves quiet in their course. With a deep exhalation the sea takes its shallows back into its lap. There is no longer a world. And all is ready for the birth of a new world. Only one swan slides away, seeking its fellows, glides over the dark-green water past the Cap of Ringabella, splitting brightness where there once was earth.

Inara Cedrins

GUNĀRS SALIŅŠ 1924–

Gunars Saliņš fled Latvia in 1944 and settled in the United States some five years later. He studied psychology at the Upsala College and the New School for Social Research and presently teaches at Union College. Saliņš was one of the influential members of the "Hells Kitchen" group. He has published three volumes of verse, and many of his poems have been translated. An English translation of his last collection, Encounters, *is soon to be published. He writes critical essays and reviews for Latvian and American publications.*

LOST IN NEW YORK

I was lost once again,
in red hair, and then
blue hair,
and green.
Buildings rustled like trees,
clusters of light swayed as if hanging from branches.
Some broke off, fell,
and burst in the streets, on cartops, like ripened berries.
Barefooted children waded through them,
women in liquid gowns of wine.
Others came from above, with baskets of grapes,
as if those were not skyscrapers up there but terraces of vine-
    yards.
They came toward me, came straight into
my arms with vineyards and skyscrapers,

and suddenly in each woman
I recognized something: eyes, lips, voice—
in each something else, some trace, some remembrance. And
   then,
as a cool hand touched me, I knew: this hand,
when a girl's, gave me the first
cluster of grapes:
               all night
her girlish form and those berries gleamed
in windows, in linden trees—yes, and in stars—
as I wandered, lost, until dawn through narrow streets
which seemed spacious, unending,
                       the very first time
I was in the city of love.

      Can it really be you live on,
      not in the graveyard's nightingales
      nor in its jasmine but
      in hundreds of beautiful women?

      In them your girlish lips
      have matured, and your eyes, your breasts:
      now our city of love is built
      of ripened flesh and the gold of vineyards.

The shimmer of loosened hair
wound in me like streets, red, blue, and green.
I found myself down in deep cellars.
They were lit by the bodies of grape girls,
radiant from wading through berries and neon signs.
In this light, on coarse-grained walls,
someone was painting his childhood dreams.
I looked more closely: incomprehensible abstracts,
but they were dripping with wine.

   Ruth Speirs

HOMECOMING

Earth under his fingernails—from it
meadow grass grew,
and from his toenails good-sized shrubs:
that's how he came back to the city after a long sleep.

Flirtatious girls
clung to his blossoming elbows,
others decorated the streets with birches, with saplings,
which grew from his armpits.

But he—he lay down
next to himself
and drank from his grassy palms,
now as though at a bar, now as though from an old well,
and had the smell of live pike for an appetizer.

"Make him say something,
make him say something,
make him sing or
say something!" we shouted.

But, turning into ears, we heard only
blossoms budding on his chest
and then a bee—or eternity?—
humming in the blossoms, or in his hair.

Interesting, but we wanted more—
and a local jazz musician, a trombonist,
bent down and tore from the sleeper's thigh
a piece of birch or alder bark,
and rolled it into a horn and
blew:

windows trembled in the bodies of skyscrapers,
wombs and breasts in the bodies of women—

as though the horn were not alder bark
but emotion, forgotten emotion.

"Enough!" a flushed, trembling blonde pleaded, "Enough!"
An unsingable song protects us all
and gives us the strength to live."
And falling to her knees, she conceived
and gave birth to a boy.

This fusion with the earth continued
three days and three nights. Like nude women
brilliant yellow-red birch trees walked through the streets—

he was home

   Inara Cedrins

SONG

In the cold my voice grew hoarse,
and one day my song
had frozen solid.

I drank hot milk with honey,
reciting a single prayer:
for the song to return—if only like
the mooing of cows or the humming of bees.

And then it happened: one night, when all
who tended me had gone,
from the waterfront slaughterhouses
cattle broke into the streets.

Thirsty, they mooed the city full. Galloping,
with their bodies and breath
they melted the snow from windows and trees,
from skyscrapers and squares.

I threw open my window—a shout
thawed my voice. From it, as from a river,

cows were drinking at noon—dipping
their warm udders in my song,

their warm udders in my song.

  Laris Saliņš

A FAUVIST LANDSCAPE WITH WOMEN

Women,
still wet,
out of clay—
with God's fingerprints, red and green, all over them.
Or God's tongueprints?
Did He just finish
licking them out of clay
with His tongue?

  Gunārs Saliņš

AT A PERFORMANCE

A temple?
Holy Communion?
The eve of the Flood?
But over the loudspeaker come stock reports, weather forecasts,
    lectures on horticulture,
and a red-haired woman in a bathrobe
dangles her legs over the balcony rail
and plays the cello—
or is it her legs that she plays?
And in the corner two young people play Ping-Pong.

In the meantime
God has stepped out by the altar
and is building

the Flood:
blue waves, green waves,
higher,
      higher,
            higher,
                  higher—
The youngsters stop their Ping-Pong match
and switch to
tiddlywinks.

On my right a Pakistani or Indian woman with beautiful skin
asks for the time
or a safety pin.
I show her the in
side of my fin,
but the cellist starts on an Irish spin.

God glances over his shoulder,
disgusted,
dismantles the waves
and takes them back to the flood warehouse.

Suddenly someone rises and shouts:
"Stop these antics—
liberate the captive nations!"

What? Was it me who shouted? Sweating
I collapse in my seat. "Oh, I see—
you too have a part in this mystery,"
marvels the Pakistani woman
with the beautiful skin.
And over the loudspeaker—stock reports, weather forecasts. But
   then at last
demonstrations begin. People come
with posters. No, with totem poles down the aisles
come the vanquished Indian tribes,
the ancient Incas along their rope bridges,
and the ancient Jatvingians, ancient Galindians, ancient Old
   Prussians, and

36   Gunārs Saliņš

dinosaurs, labidosaurs,
alosaurs, trachodons,
diplodoci, triceratops,
Tyrannosaurus rex—

they come in procession
with the Jatvingians, with the Galindians, with the Old Prussians
("It's kind of fun to be extinct,"*
a ghastly diplodocus in passing whispers in my ear)—
and they disappear where God disappeared.
And over the loudspeaker—stock reports, weather forecasts,
   lectures on horticulture.
From the cello, from the balcony rail
the cries of fish, laughter of earthworms, twittering of snakes.
And the Pakistani woman walks around and distributes
forgiveness of sins? mercy? the flesh of God?
                                  I sense
through my leg, through my shinbone, someone is ringing me
(as if by telephone), and then at my ear I hear
a dreaming skull—

                    waters mix with sounds,
                    fire mixes with stone,
                    hills with the sun, with the moon, with the stars,
                    plants with the air—

A dreaming skull.

   Gunārs Saliņš

ABYSS

Deeper and deeper
we vanished into the gorge, vanished
into the abyss
of autumn leaf,
scent and fruit.

*From Ogden Nash, *The Private Dining Room and Other Verses.*

You let go my hand
and trotted ahead
downward amidst the fruit,
the gold,
the red.

Then you reclined in leaves,
hands around your knees,
arms around your black skirt.
Were you breathing fruit?
Were you waiting for me?

I caught up, filled up
your lap with fruit—
blushing and golden
you surrendered—
the immaculate conception.

Deeper and deeper
we vanished into the gorge, vanished
into the abyss
of autumn leaf,
scent and fruit.

Laris Saliņš

DANCER

My arms around you, I feel
ripples of dancing.
Dance, oh dance
and gird yourself with nothing
but my arms.

Velta Sniķere

RAIN

(in Stockholm)

I head into the rain.
I walk and walk in this rain. It is
impassable. Impassable
groves of rain, woods of rain, primeval forests of
rain. I've lost my way.
I've passed back through my life. Through my own
birth. Through my mother's flesh.
Further back. Further. Where am I?
Rain. Rain. Impassable.

   Bitīte Vinklers

A MUSEUM PIECE

In the ancient sunstone
I felt the heat of the ancient sun.
And I came to life.
I started to dance.
I was the god of this altar.
      When I had finished—still out of breath, still godlike—
I put my arm around my beloved
ready to move on.
          But the museum guard
stopped us. "You don't mean to," he asked her, pointing at me,
"you don't mean to take this exhibit with you?"
             And nothing could convince him,
neither documents nor her despair.
He called another guard, and then the two of them
got me (I still can't figure out how)
inside the sunstone.

By now I've been here I can't tell how long.
Occasionally my beloved comes to visit me, and when the
   guards aren't looking

she touches the stone and whispers,
"Darling . . ."

And that's the way we live now

Gunārs Saliņš

RETURNING HOME

(Latvia, 1976)

Receiving us
he trembled, he shimmered, intoxicated and intoxicating—
    he was
currants, cherries, strawberries, plums,
tomatoes, parsley, dill—
      from private gardens,
      from private plots?
That whole day and night
he nourished us of himself,
and toward dawn it was he, fermented by then, that we drank.
But at sunrise, when our legs no longer obeyed us,
he rose, and on his shoulders and elbows of wine he carried us
home.

When we awoke, he himself had fallen into a deep sleep,
in the corner of the garden, on the ground.
Frightened, we saw he was no longer
vines, or berries, or wine:
he was moldering earth. He lay
decaying within himself, already dead,
with roots of trees and vines
across him and his hair matted with the leaves of many autumns.
There were roots through the hollows of his eyes and these roots
    coiled deeper,
through the hollowed eyes of others—roots entwined with
    barbwire

piercing his eyes in the sleep of death.

What am I saying! At that moment he woke,
and sensing us leaning over him—silhouetted against the towers
   of Riga and of New York—he rose,
and in rising gathered himself together and became again
flesh,
flesh and fruit and
berries and wine. And again he
trembled,
he shimmered,
intoxicated and intoxicating,
for one more day—one more, as short as life, one more
summer day home

   Bitīte Vinklers

A CONCERT IN THE DOM CATHEDRAL, RIGA

Hands. A pair of hands. Severed
on the rails in Vorkuta twenty years ago,
fitfully these hands are playing the organ,
the hands alone

while someone else, with frostbitten amputated feet,
with feet alone,
is running along the organ pedals for twenty years now,
is running from the Arctic Circle
home

   Bitīte Vinklers

MOMENTS

We're startled—
as if birds, flowers, stars
and our own faces, laughter and trembling

were falling through us—
as if we already were
fleshless flesh
with bones of sun.

But that's only a moment. No,
we're sitting opposite one another in a crowded cafe
with faces, with laughter—
                                        with trembling
In flowers,
birds,
stars.

    Laris Saliņš

I WOKE TO A HORSE'S NEIGHING

I woke to a horse's neighing—
through my hotelroom window, left open that night,
leaned a horse's
head.
So Riga still had dray horses?
Amazed, I propped myself up on an elbow.
What to serve him—black bread? a pickle?
But then it hit me—he just might be
a secret agent in disguise!
                                        He neighed again, more intelligibly:
"Calm down,
I'm not from the CIA or KGB. Don't you know me? —Rick.
We parted thirty-three years ago—when they shipped me
to Volkhov."
                        Rick! Of course!
Only with a deeper voice, and the looks
of a horse.
"It's easier this way," he neighed, muzzle on the sill.
After the war, dispatched to the north for a "rest."

Upon his return at last, no father, mother, sister, no sweetheart
   anymore.
So, then—he had become a drayman.
       A drayman?
I peered at him closely—no, a horse like any other horse!
"Well," he lightly neighed, "it's how you look at things.
Besides, there are advantages—for instance, their mikes
can't pick up horseplay . . ."
And he meaningfully glanced at my ceiling.
So, we horsed around.
About old times.
And so on.
And on and on.
At parting we drank a toast
of some good old "horse schnapps."
                          "Till next time," he neighed,
and, horseshoes clicking, trotted away
through Old Riga at dawn—
                          a horse like any other horse

   Bitūte Vinklers

THE CHERRY ORCHARD IN SOMEONE'S HEAD

(a séance with a director)

He's sitting straight in front of us, in half darkness.
The back of his head is shaved, as if from a recent brain operation,
and through the pallid skin we discern just barely noticeable
movement: A woman holding a candle feels her way
among furniture covered over with pale cloth—she finds the sofa
and lies down, the burning candle still in her hand.
And through her sleep as if through a window
dawns a cherry orchard.
In an instant her head is filled with singing birds.
And her breasts slide through the cherry orchard

●

The sound of a muted horn,
still deeper in her head, deeper in the orchard.
And a moth-eaten student
through moth-eaten spectacles peers at me.
"I don't understand
my own thoughts," he says,
and dejected sits down
and sways as if in a hammock in the fading sound in her head.
Her straw hat twists
and falls to the floor like a
face

●

Someone is strumming a mandolin
in her freckles.
—He's alive! she feels. He's alive!—what a miracle!
Just the day before yesterday he was dead

●

Standing up she staggers with the candle in her hand—
something beneath her feet has been auctioned.
A burst of hysterical laughter, and then she runs—
several times she runs around life
that is no more.

The candle goes out.
So the performance is over?

P.S. It's all so theatrical, I say to myself,
       and yet true.
       The director turns around and says to me,
       "Truth *is* theatrical."
       And his own face flickers like the flame of a candle
       and goes out

       Bitīte Vinklers

44   Gunārs Saliņš

HER SONG ON THE WAY TO THE SCAFFOLD

(Poulenc's Dialogues des Carmélites
  at the Metropolitan Opera)

I

She approaches us on song
that reaches into this blackness like a white cross—
she sings this cross into the darkness around her.
In fear of death still singing she sinks to her knees,
in fear of death she lies down in the cross she has sung and stretches
    her arms—
and she is nailed to it by sudden
silence

II

She sings again,
rising, she sings a lattice of crosses around herself—
she has sung herself into a cage.
It separates her from the world.
It protects as it imprisons.
And she falls silent—in wonder that she has been saved.
But the lattice of crosses she has sung—at that moment it rises,
shimmering it ascends above her to heaven. And again
she is alone and unprotected
at the foot of the scaffold

III

Her final singing—so clear
we can see through it, as she climbs the scaffold steps.
We can see death transcended.
And across it—life transcended.
A cross—transparent and light—shines through her voice.
Transparent unto everlasting joy.

And then the guillotine falls

Bitīte Vinklers

STORM IN THE STREETS

A storm in the streets—
slamming the door behind us,
it hurled us together against the wall
that reeled like a woman
in dread and passion,
like you.

"Let's run!" cried your mouth
as you forced it away from mine.
But the storm tossed it back
like a scarlet leaf
at my cheek,
my eyelids,
my throat.

Then you ran—but the street surged about you,
splashed you with lights torn from lamps and from windows
and, rising underneath you,
knocked you over—
                and, with a wave,
          you were swept
    back
into my arms.

                The street enfolded us
                like the sea. Buildings drifted
                past as they sank
                locked in embrace
                with their lights.

Ruth Speirs

BAIBA BIČOLE   1931–

Baiba Bičole was born in Riga, where her mother was a poet and critic, and her father a literary historian and critic of great distinction. She left Latvia in 1944 to escape the Soviet occupation and later came to the United States. She is married to Ilmārs Rumpēteris, one of the foremost Latvian graphic artists. Bičole's first volume of poetry, published in 1966, won the Zinaida Lazda Prize, a prestigious award for poetry outside Latvia. Her three additional volumes of poetry have been well received.

AUTUMN IN THE HILLS

Rust-colored horses have cantered through the forests,
the orange of the trails
is kicked up,
firs in the silvered snow of distant hills,
the fields glittering frost.

With loudly crunching footsteps
I steal close to the forest's red apple trees;
the fruit has a knife's cold and sharp
flesh, bitterness
cuts into my tongue,

the iron palms of the wind
press my eyes closed,
gouge to the bone.

   Inara Cedrins

AT A PAINTING

These sisters in clashing colors
pressed into one display window,
arguing and struggling with teeth gritted—
the hand that created
and now rests at peace
they'd like to pluck out
like a weed root,

but they're like fish
beneath a lid of ice;
they move and don't move away,
they toss and don't pull away,
they scream, and their language
is transparent bubbles
in transparent water.

Inara Cedrins

TWO PORTRAITS

1

The street in darkness. A door.
He goes in.
Inside, a stairway
like scattered teeth,
clocks with jumbled insides,
the hearth deep in dust,
forgotten languages,

he flees—
that's not reality, that isn't life!
—He throws himself along the crumbling road
toward wakening,

the street ends in a brick wall.
Clay fist on forehead.

2
Help! Help!

> But the cry
> like a late unpicked fruit
> soft with rottenness
> fell to the grass.

The tree trunk girds itself for winter.
Along the branch was clearly visible
the tangled mass of an abandoned nest,
and in the compost heap of leaves
transformation has just begun.

Inara Cedrins

MY EYES

I
My eyes are lanterns and wineglasses,
and my shoulders of warm brown wood;
from my every finger unreels
a soft, fluffy dizziness.

II
What emptied eyes!
My length is pale as marble and cool;
someone strums something
on my dry veins—
how the palms rattle, applauding!
Between us is a white table
like a desert of snow.

III
I am red, tossing candlelight
and the tablecloth, streaked with bloodveins;
I am the hunting dog with steaming, lolling tongue,
I am the fox hunter in a red jacket,

a mare skittishly highstrung
and the call of the horn—
and then suddenly I gallop
straight into mirrors,
and all surfaces and levels
                              part
and I become that
which I gaze back upon.

   Inara Cedrins

IN EVENING

Throwing back its head, the sun momentarily
steeps its bright hair still
in the water, in the next instant
it has drawn back,
        bound a violet knot about its head,
        become an old woman with bowed shoulders
        hurrying, shrinking
greyer and greyer;
steps over the sill of the horizon
and disappears—

        but we with eyes still dazed
        look into the water, into hollow depths,
        canals, rivers and all the lakes—
        no, those are the delicate frizzling rays
        of tiny stars
        that frolic toward us,
        and at the forest's edge dances an apparition
                                of phosphor.

   Inara Cedrins

THE ARRIVAL

When we re-enter the street
we find it frosted over.
Frightening to walk past whitened bushes
putting out fingers
to feel
the newly come ice age's
first fragments.

> Windows made blank
> signs of hiding? Symbol of giving in?
> Pale frost flowers.
> Faces hang in the glass.

> > I become aware
> > of buildings like dinosaurs
> > beginning to lean
> > not toward awakening
> >   but to sleep,
> >   I say nothing

> > the crooked script of my footprints
> > is surely more clear
> > than my mouth's stammering whisper

> > my lips
> > two chips of ice
> > fall and shatter;
> > alone in the echo,
> > crazed, a woman
> > flees.

Inara Cedrins

LANDSCAPES OF AN HOUR

1

the battered cup of morning
my lips are long gullies
brown rust ripples down

2

the plowshare turns under
my garland of tangled hair
shrieking

3

spoked stance
the brownish crablike plow
not a mare

4

green frog lake
red shins of sunset
parting the reeds

5

the monkey sleep clambers in the creepers
howls with joy
when I fall

6

across the white weave of sheets
my length draws
a nude

7

rummaging in rubbish
a loaf of crumbs
stained translation of dream

Inara Cedrins

ANCIENT MOTHER

She is bowl and spoon at the same time,
dipped into, ladled from
by husband, children and household;
she's a steaming light and floury

                            potato,
white milk and tiny groats,
the yellow eye of butter
and dark green, pungent green onion;
she's the table and she is the bed
from which, edging through centuries
the tribe clambers out and rises,
with its writing in folk song and plaid.

   Inara Cedrins

RAIN AT HAYING TIME

The storm grows distant. Still reluctantly
lifting eyelids, clouds
look back with lightning eyes,
and in the distance thunder rumbles
like a closing door.

Clean, lengthy and sorrowful
into the wept-over fields
evening wades,
hands full
of drowned flowers.

   Inara Cedrins

A QUIVERING SHUDDER

A quivering shudder ran through my limbs,
a whole handful of glittering red ants
were thrown into my panes by sunset.
Window vaults like crosses,
congealed resin catching
                              wings and feet.
Lightly and silent as thieves
                              colors steal away,
and I pale, carding in my hands
sheets of grey
          ash.

          My bed is a hundred-year-old
                              woman,
          what veined, sinewed feet!
          Her ribs and backbone
                              press
          through all the blankets;
          she's become miserly and
          keeps all dreams
                              to herself.
          Night enmeshes me
                              like a sieve.

Inara Cedrins

UNLIKE SISTERS

Unlike sisters. Days. One radiant in coloring
and one shuffling on flat webbed feet.
Auburn-haired beauty with lush brown eyes and apple cheeks—
and the gaunt wife, rubbed down to paleness.
Every night there's a funeral, the clarity of dream

54   Baiba Bičole

giving the very tactile image of the departed.
And yet in the mornings through grave wreaths,
                                        ribbons
new vaults and furrows checker the land,
newborn shoots extend and
                        scream

   Inara Cedrins

THE STRANGE WOMAN

Long, stretched-out forms,
                changing shapes—
she was like a woman in a carnival trick mirror—
oh, how fiercely her husband loved her
and sensed with bewildered questioning
that his wife had no border
to press against
to measure up to,
        like a serpent he wove himself
        into her ways, her valleys
                        silty rivers,
                (while the big toe of her foot
                put a furrow in the seaside sand,
                her lap threw off the shrieking child
                with the spoon of life still in clenched fist,
                but her eyes
                under half-open lids
                dreamed,
                        long, long highroads
                                dreamed
                        and remembered nothing).

Sea mist. Fog.
—To some there appeared
the trembling nakedness of flesh

and the quick lift of nipples
beneath some hand—

> but she held out long, a grain of salt,
> saltwaters' glittering belts,
> held severely to
> the fast days'
> refreshment—
> > then one day
> > > unexpectedly
> > fishbones sprinkled in the palm,
> > scales tumbled awry
> > > brilliance of neither thaler, nor tear—
> > in the white all-illuminated
> > > > fist of apathy—
> > > suddenly she understood
> > > it all came to nothing
> the sea rushed out
> boat belly up
> net among the algae
> fish eyes upon breasts—
> > but from shore to shore
> > peace
> > > like on the seventh
> > > or
> > > sabbath day.

Inara Cedrins

SORCERY

1

My hand passes through you
to feel in the vertebrae of your backbone
soft buds of a sudden springtime,

56   Baiba Bičole

my hair winds itself around your heart
—little pillow of brown fern—
and sometimes, when I shift,
you grow restless.
The toes of my feet are in your palms
no longer able to write,
only to rake through sand—
        let's leave as a signature
        this communal
        foot-finger imprint.

    2

Arching my left eyebrow
I loop it around your right eye
and instill small mischiefs.
Just now you complain, that there
scratching bites of insects among the grass clods,
that behind glass panes the landowner's wife is cooking oilcakes
and will not vouchsafe you even a crumb,
only thick smoke from the cook's underarms
braids itself into your eyelashes—
        I'll kiss you away from reality,
        you'll believe anything.

   Inara Cedrins

SOUTHERN SKIES

    1

The winds, with bared loins
stride
through the middle of the street,
and their rising strength
is felt in my every pore,
the breadth of their breathing
in my chest.

2

I discover southern skies overhead
and lift them in my hand, and feel—
                           snow melting,
                    the brown honey of mud
                    drips between my fingers,
                    revived ants itch
                    the lines on my palm.
The aged grove sounds out as though blowing pipes,
tiny fine drumming sounds
long icicles
     dripping.

3

I carry your light, weightless bones over the grass,
you need no urn, nor heavy marker stone—
standing about in the April sunlight
your green children
with their finespun hair
swing forth a mild Alleluja
and I feel no sorrow.

   Inara Cedrins

OLAFS STUMBRS   1931–

Olafs Stumbris left Latvia at age thirteen for Germany as the Soviet armies advanced westwards. He emigrated to the United States in 1950 and settled in Los Angeles, where he attended college and in the late fifties became involved in the beatnik movement. Stumbris has published three collections of poems and has received the Zinaida Lazda Prize.

VARIATIONS

(An Attempt on the Life of the Traditional Quaträin)

1

She smiles me the frost of October,
her eyes—dark, ice-cold wine.
Without warning, a murderer sober
cuts neatly my throat and i die.

Dead. People stare at me stonily.
Transfiguration. I'm Strauss.
From her eyes such a small sip only . . .
"Is a Doctor Johnson in the house?"

He is and he says: "Cold and sober,
ye shall never again have to die.
For therapy
in your mirror daily

practice the frost of October
and abstain from the wine and the Why."

2

She smiles me the frost of October
and—why does it make me drunk?—
her eyes, never calm, never sober,
    blink just once
and i am an elephant's trunk.

    Curled up spring-tight with desire,
    i am a spinning grey hoop,
    i dance her through desert, through mire—
        Tough little witch,
    she hides in a chicken coop.

The rooster alights like a candle,—
glowing sunrise comb upon white.
With his beak he unfastens her sandals
    and, afraid to rhapsodize early,
just cackles her not to take flight.

    She explains how this magic-prone, hoop-like,
    how this trunk-minus-beast brought her woe.
    He assures her. Bent gracefully stoop-like,
        she lays him an egg,
    then scratches in soil with bare toes.

But i in the yard forsaken
all day loop the coop, loop the coop.
A witch can't be tamed or taken:
    when sky lays the moon
she'll come and play with her hoop.

3

She smiles me the frost of October,
and from floor long icicles grow
a pipe organ wintry, sober—

My preacher, awakened by the cold
                    sits down
and starts a stately tune slowly.

        She's young. She would hate his recital.
        She's pretty. With passion he plays.
        All keys are ice. Joy is triteness.
        More mirthless, more merciless message
                    fingers search.
        Engrossed, he's a black pendulum swaying

She can't see, she can't hear what he's doing,
my preacher with icicle tunes:
she sees a man: not a ruin,
        just not so young. If he'd smile
                    he would not
look so wrinkled and blue like a prune.

    4
She smiles me the frost of October,
but how does that cruel mouth taste?
A sudden explorer, a prober,
i enter her wasteland.

Neon stares down in surprise.
Cars dim their lights and rush by.
(The taste is both fresh and wise—
between mod NOW! moody WHY?)

Eyes smile. No more frost. Exclamation:
"You are very young!"—Why not?
Poet's reward: time's stationary.
As you grow older i'll become
                    your pink, plump-kneed tot.

Don't laugh! you are my poem
thought up with this morning street.
I'll fold you both when i'm going,

stick inside my coat pocket,
                and take you home with me.

My wife won't mind. Understanding,
she'll smooth your creases and then,
with help of thumbtacks and rubber bands,
                fasten the street, the kiss, the you
on the less cluttered wall of my den.

   5
She smiles me the frost of October—
Palms drop coconuts, cancel dates,
and an elderly claustrophobe
        peacefully crawls inside
            a ladies' wristwatch
                chronically
                late.

Creaking sadly, Earth stops on its axis.
Seas stretch out in the sun to be dried.
No hoods. No states. No taxes.
Death turns in his scythe. He's fired.

Though ground thin, the sky is still up.
Brown mountain rock crumbles into plains.
The New Father Time, still up,
i stroll with my brandless new cane,
        unhurried,
              i stroll the New Eternity—
                  tup, tup, tup . . .

(*Originally written in English*)

WINTER

In the clearing, a tree against the sky
like a charcoal-drawn silhouette on a sheet of paper.
I go closer, bend down, squeeze snow in my palms and throw.

Snowball crashes against bark and sticks there.
One more, once more—
two birds reluctantly take wing.
Stars flicker on. Night comes.
Fingers already boiled lobster color.
Night comes.
Dreadful, sparking, freezing night comes.

Inara Cedrins

SONG AT A LATE HOUR

Sometime at night you'll look for me
in the mole's narrow burrow,
but I'll just chuckle softly
and hide at the deepest end.
        I'll look up at you;
        you'll stand black against the stars
        but be unable to reach me in that darkness—
        neither your pain, nor your palm.
And I'll whisper to the mole: "Landlord
do you see? That's my soul—
returned at last
when this burrow has become all and plenty.

Inara Cedrins

ASPENS IN THE WIND

Light and pale as dandelion fluff,
that day aspen souls roamed the winds
looking for a place in which to be born.

One clung for a long time in your hair, above the right temple.
Even these youngest souls must have their fantasies!

You walked beside me completely lightly
with a sportively crooked aspen seed above your right ear,
absolutely unaware
that in your hair swung
a great green tree with
bird nests and hanging feeders,
a great white tree with
winter's stiffened loneliness in its branches,
a tree with the tragedies of boys' torn trousers, with
hearts and initials carved in its bark, with
its top split by lightning—

perhaps not for others,
but to you
this tree was very
becoming.

Inara Cedrins

CONFESSION

1
all is
eroticism, and those who haven't
their own car will call you to walk in the night beach
darkness, and those who don't cerebralize
poems will say: "but stay the night with
me," and those who are ashamed to lift your checked
skirts, will instead twist an eyebrow
upward, and this too is a way in which nature celebrates
its victory. But later at night, when the darkness
of blood sways the bed like a friendly, nervous
wave, all we joyous alike
creatures will at last achieve
peace: some in long searched for arms, some—
in others. And then? In that

64   Olafs Stumbrs

darkness, all
hands, like proverbial
cats, will be uniformly
grey, with morning still
distant—

   2
spring is not the time
of poets, For instance, in winter each
evening I drink to my beloved's
burial, and those melodies I know
flow from lily stems, the coolest
clarinetist can only be envious. But in April, May, when
yellow tulips
burn even in the dead-looking beach
sand, when every
wave leaves ashore small
fish, which sing loudly with rounded mouths of
springtime in the blossoming algae—then I really feel completely
out of place: a laughable leftover snowman, having forgotten
to thaw in time, when the sun's golden
mouth pressed against the eyes of coal
fervently—

   3
the green of the hills is eaten off by a yellow
cow, in narrow streams fish swirl up
silk; dancing a private Dance
Macabre, my proud one
permits the shadow of sunflowers to kiss the damp
hollows of her knees, but I accept all
humbly, murmuring something about the yet withheld
summer—

   4
lately the preponderance of girls
are only a way in which to lose
memory: exaggeratedly large, rosy

erasers, that rub against me until again
some aged, drawn clumsily
with lipstick
profile has been extinguished from my one-page
soul, until I am again
clean, empty, cool—

5

it'd be nice to talk through the night in a Chinese
Mandarin tongue with a slant-eyed old
man, better to watch
the world fall asleep under a blue raven's wing, best
to stand again three feet tall at the slate kitchen
sink, scrubbing from fingers the dark
stains stubbornly left from plucked dandelions'
milk—

Inara Cedrins

UNDERLININGS

Sometimes the poem doesn't want to flow onto the page:
an ink blue, self-drawn cloud
it floats
above the page somewhere in the region of the heading,
and beneath it is a white, solitary desert.
No one manages to cross it: there's no road, no guidepost.

But if it were to rain?

Perhaps we'd see long, decorative camel caravans
with strong spices,
with fragrant bondswomen on the journey from India,
we'd see New York's 5th Avenue in summer rain:
asphalt and the backs of hurrying people steaming warmly,
four synthetically dressed women in gigantic hairstyles
nuzzled in

to one narrow telephone booth;
we'd see the old Daugava spruces
in their most gorgeous
plumage;
then just one short ("but the young man won't come up")
Schiller fragment
pressed into Latvia's old
orthography;
two pike
(oh the green one with the wave and that other
with a slice of lemon);
we'd see you, me,
ourselves;
perhaps some
words of sense;
the world's sweetest smelling
lindens—

But no one knows.
It only drizzled.

Inara Cedrins

SPRING NIGHT

Winds come from the darkened hills
and bring the scent of thawing earth
to this city, where earth is so deep in stone
that it will never be warmed.

Winds come from the darkened hills,
from spruce thickets, where snow melts slowly.
They drive old papers down the valley
and play with shadows in the pale bulbs.

Inara Cedrins

LETTER TO MY ENCHANTRESS

These days are heavy.
Storm clouds hover in the air, and the heart wishes to toss
          a spark upward, but can't.
And burns slowly of itself.

                         *   *   *

You were somewhere, I know;
I looked for you in the field, but plucked yellow dandelion fluff.
I looked for you in the forest, but caught a red squirrel in a spruce.
I looked for you in a cheap city room, but came upon
                    the evening star in the dark window.
Now I possess much. I should be fortunate,
but
I carelessly twist flowers in my hands,
I feed the squirrel in a cardboard box,
I open the window and allow visitors to smell my
                              evening star,
and grow downcast once in a while:
" . . . You were somewhere . . ."

                         *   *   *

These days are heavy.
Blood boils in the veins like wormwood tea, and bitter
          spirits climb into the head and tinge the brain
          green.

                         *   *   *

       . . . the brain, eh? . . .
Soon it'll be winter, and the lake will sleep frozen in the park
     between frosty shores like a gooseberry
     jelly in a white bowl.
And I'll slide through the days upon greenish ice
                    and twitch at my own shadow
In the evening at home I'll make my squirrel hot coffee
               of ground dandelion leaves,

but I'll press the evening star into the palm of a boy, who
                              brings the newspaper up to the apartment.
      . . . the brain, eh? . . .

                    **   **   **

These days are heavy.
Beauty scorches in the heat of blood, and longings are tossed
                              to life like tips.
But life remains,
remains and grows in strength every moment.
The heart will soon toss a hot spark to the heavy
            sky, and it seems that my world will still
            glint back once in that light.
You surely existed.

   Inara Cedrins

ON THE STREET

I gazed into the scarlet evening skies, appealing to
    the sinking sun, which had today presented earth with
    your shadow.

Not far from me it caressed the fortunate sidewalk.

And I went carefully around the asphalt quadrant,
    as though it were smoked glass, which would break
    with my steps.

   Inara Cedrins

THE MERMAID FORMED OF SAND

While out for a walk along the shore,
I accidentally trod upon
her prettily arranged tail.
She was a beautiful mermaid:

hair cut in a style popular in Riga in the thirties
and (we don't write lies if reality is stronger),
it was real, green, seaweed.
The aforementioned sand creation's artist, being of the people,
and not thirsting after unknown distances,
had created (after foreign models) breasts as well.
These, some boy in rosy pants,
(oh, how to get this across to you?)
as yet not understanding the high-breasted ideal,
had just decorated with colored paper flags.
So a split could be felt
between both honored heights—or (as it seemed to him)
                                    massive fortresses
where a group of tiny stick figures stood,
figuring out, it seemed, with which to enlist.

Surrealism on the Baltic shore!
Critics, here one dares not be passive!
Draw the flags of storm up onto the masts in time!
In a few years the boy will wear blue—and later the Academy's—
                                    long pants.
Come rather to his assistance
with ideo- and pedagogical might!
Demonstrate an ant to him—
it lives brilliantly in its realism.
Teach him the rhinoceros—
for surely the monumental dare not waver.
But above all things
        drill into him some of the recent guidelines
so that he recognizes rigidity in time.
Today, with mother or governess,
let's cry to him only: "Hands off the breasts!"
It'll only be warning to pause to the boy.
The time will come—he'll teach girls
                        without difficulty.

Inara Cedrins

AINA KRAUJIETE   1923–

Aina Kraujiete emigrated to the United States in 1949. By professional training a medical researcher, having studied in Frankfurt, Germany, and at the Sloan-Kettering Institute, Kraujiete worked at various research institutes until 1976. Now she devotes her time to creative writing and editorial duties with the Latvian literary magazine Jaunā Gaita. *She is married to the Latvian journalist and editor Viktors Neimanis. Kraujiete has published five volumes of poetry, and her work has been translated into English and Lithuanian and set to music by the Latvian composer Arnolds Sturms.*

FROM A BARTERED PARADISE

In March
daffodils will not come into bloom here
as in other places, when spring's in the garden and in
                                        flowerpots. Here will drip
only the roofs

from morning till night.
Therefore it's not good to reach after colors whose
brightness is more brilliant than lush bougainvillea

blossoms.
In winding side streets they've clung to every building
instead of clusters of burgeoning

berry and fruit like cheap
candy box covers, for this is a corrupt illusion

city.
Those are poster
colors. With unabashed light they sparkle, wave
and seek
lovers of nonexistent joy,
and everyone, who perhaps wishes to sin
they'll entice
here into a side

street. Youthfully timid and with the shine of neon letters
as though of the promised land's gleam on cheek, he'll choke
                                        coins in damp
palm and slide note after note
through the cashier's glass cage,
impatiently longing to enter the building, in which his strength
drawn by visions of topless dancers

will be cheated—
for this is such a quarter.
In March
daffodils don't bloom here,
but at times from a bartered paradise
someone who's been pushed out

hangs.

Inara Cedrins

VAGABOND'S ARISING

—slide and—
                        pass on
past the door
his wavering carefree steps.

raising up dust in the corridor.
                    Come to rest—
to reverberate again in the night like pebbles
on the stairs and at the entrance
to the city, upon which as on an immense sink
ordinary people flow together
as flood waters whirlpooling
buildings, skyscrapers, underground regions,
and then rinse out again to go forward on the streets.

In the hustling crowd like a button torn off a coat
underfoot for everyone, unnecessary, he goes sensing
—tonight he should be far from this place—

but all his senses
yearn for strange smells and sounds, strange pleasures,
leaning to the sensual-like grass to the rain,
and not able
to turn away any longer from lit window—
as though by some miracle
seeing in it

the Oberammergau Passion Play
or sinning Franciscan monks at vespers
or perhaps
something else. He doesn't know—
                    will the bells ring
of Christ arising or toll his own death;
if only he could
go in, where there's light and
                    stay—

In the morning, when droplets of rain
spray like dew on
his face (yellow and sour as a lemon)
he awakens—
not even on a bench,

but in place, where in the cracked asphalt of pavement
the damp tar will not allow a single shoot of grass

—where no daffodils will bloom in March—

and the holy morning's rumbled over by everyday steps.

Inara Cedrins

TWO SISTERS

One was crystal,
the other—red clay.

One danced in crystal-lit halls,
the other, upon her knees,
raked out potatoes, whole.

War parted them at once and left
underfoot for each, completely different earth.

On her toes, light as prism-rays from crystal chandeliers
one sister danced in the halls of state.

The other, heavy as clay
remained at the boundaries of home,
always frightened by barred wagons
already set on the rails.

Crystal with time shattered and wasted away in dust.
Clay, long fired, survived long and hard years.

Inara Cedrins

THE BRIDE

she didn't know whether to weep
or rejoice when from the limousine
a black-liveried chaffeur leapt to open the door

74   Aina Kraujiete

before her begonia-pot decorated
vine-wound
porch

—he had returned returned returned

damask woven with shiny leaves
curtained the door at which she hid
she didn't know to which side
to turn her eyes or
whether it would be to cry
as before or to rejoice

—he had returned returned

through the lattice of fingers covering face she watched
on the porch the sun was above the dahlias
all the words that had been hoarded for the arrival
and laid at night beside pillow
words she tried to rearrange in her mind
but like porcelain
brittle and thin
they were worn away
and sagged unspoken
crumbled under the tongue's heaviness

—he had returned

thick vine tendrils
the wind wove into neighbors' cage-like windows
wives' headscarves fluttered and around the corner
children chewing bubble gum sullenly watched—
he had returned in his
limousine and (probably) with money
but already since the Sunday it had rained all morning
she had no longer been called the abandoned bride

and in unhealable weeping
damask curtains allowed to smother
the untimely unawaited joy

   Inara Cedrins

THE ARRIVAL

Climbing through the wind
the green hop rustles
and the tasselled oats swish

—as though the splendid
Queen of Sheba, her veils held up
by flower stalks, were walking by

—as though from above
her heaving breast a reflecting jewel threw
a broken-rayed sun onto the grass

—as though hot, heavy and honeyed, a bumblebee
hummed, but blood
spurned to fresh ardor
by the ancient queen's nearness

—as though, with her,
sent
to the pale harvester of oats

at high noon
in the green rush of hop
were the gentle majesty—

                              death.

   Ilze Šķipsna

CITY GIRLS

The city's pale-blooded
girls stretch up high
in windows and
with fingers delicate as Fijian chrysanthemum petals

76   Aina Kraujiete

toss them
shut and open.

Their figures wouldn't leave gentle impressions in beach
sands, and goose-down softness does not await them
in a twosome joy.

Nervous, as though disturbed from over-sure dream, they
feel of woven flowers in the curtains and listen tensely

how steps reverberate
scuffing
on the stairs—
                    stride and—
                              slide off

past the door. Passionless
their mouths like pale
thistle blossoms stick softly to the palm,
so as not to become loud.

Unnecessary
to themselves, and useless to the never dark boulevard,
the city's pale-blooded
girls wilt in the windows and
toss them
shut and open.

Inara Cedrins

WITH THE PARROT OF PEACE

I know—paradise
is green
with giant low-branched fig trees. I don't care
how it really happened—
how Adam got his clothing leaf.
I know only a paradise

monstrously green. Soon
I'll be accompanied to where there're only white
chalk walls; in the center
among metal-wrought grated
tall windows
I'll draw not a plump dove in flight with
palm branch, but paradise's apple
in the crooked beak of a bright-feathered bird,
for I am an artist par excellence.

Every ray's reflection in pocket mirror
causes me
to think of paradise and
never of jungles, where a parrot chattering of peace
perches over orchids.

I am an artist—my color satchel
is full of unstarted tubes for chasing starry rainbows
but not the slightest challenge
of brushes. Look,
though I see others turn from me or flee,
I know how to paint well with hands,
with only sweeps of the fingers, not to let fall
ever a streak of color
(this in place of all twelve bride's
sisters, for they too did not appear at the wedding).
And why trail
between altars and courtroom,
if one knows how to draw birds, apple, grass

in thought. Only don't question me! I come
from jungle (or some similar place) with grass
trimmed, along whose edges trumpet war-marchers,
intruding into places where sit-ins protest
against cats, vaccinations
(and much else); peace rallies.

I desire peace without coveting manifestos.

Inara Cedrins

78   Aina Kraujiete

SHEETS LIFTED OFF

Sheets lifted off like bats
night stole over the edges of the bed
swaying darkness ran
to and over
the sleeper. Who curled into a ball.
A cone of brilliance hurtled through the window—

"Wake!" I called to myself, and completely—
to my ears—waded into the sun.

Inara Cedrins

IN CHALK ROOMS

        let all the walls
        about me be green
        like a whole harvest
        of summer's meadows

walls like light
    sliding through green bottle-glass
walls like forest
    moss-grown and damp
walls like mouldy
    cheese on a knife
and walls like frogs
    so cool and loud
walls with gentleness
    like budding leaves
walls of juiciness
    as of chopped turnip tops
walls in that tone
    in which rain soaks moss
and yellowed like cabbage
    butterflies assuming a cocoon

walls hard and green
    corrugated wet
encompassing me
    as have only woods and waters.

    but the world listens
    to me as to a gnat's song
    though I suffer terrible
    famine for greenness

Inara Cedrins

HIGH NOON

Neither battle drums
nor trumpets of victory
nor the bell in cemetery chapel
would perturb me as much
as a lizard's silent flight from the sun
    signalling
        high noon
           of the summer.

Was I to know
under wild laurel bushes in bloom
I would be overcome
while in slumber
by the aroma of wilted petals
(and my song just begun).

Aina Kraujiete

IN THE FIELD

And again the grasshopper sounds without sadness,
a bird fills the sky, even to the earth, with song.
At a tower's distance
a city wrinkles the horizon.
Here the city dweller blossoms as a flower in the field
and along with the blossoms, fades, as though plowed down
in the first haying
swath.

   Inara Cedrins

EPITAPH

If sorrow could be
thrown into the river like stones
today it would transcend shores
with flood-like strength—

              for we are weighted down
              like stones mute with sorrow.

   Inara Cedrins

PILGRIMS OF LOVE

Where in a violet sky
huge stars like topazes glimmer
among leaves of palm
folded as for benediction,
where the siroccos subside
into whispers that stir
the sun-bleached jacaranda blossoms,
where the ocean rolls
all through the night

Aina Kraujiete   81

the same lazy wave
like a girl rinsing her hair,
and Orion throws its glow
among silvery fish
in the warm waters—
over Orion's belt
as over a bridge will pass
not many, but two
pilgrims of love.

    Astrīde Ivaska

FLOODS

Curving lions among thick woolen stalks
and masterfully weaving silken rivers—
she sewed the day through
on a wall tapestry, sitting at the garret window
more obedient than medieval virgins
in chastity belts.

Evenings
she loosened her hair and bodice
and, reddened by her bath like a young
witch,
enfolded in a shiny clinging kimono,
polished her nails

And when he came, not suddenly
clamoring, but quietly—as promised
to only stay the night—
breathless rain rushed about the building.

Caught in the tail of the storm
the last slow drops
of morning still dripped,

and she settled on the windowsill to further float
between stabbing wool, the shimmering silks

Hair, which streaming in the darkness
had slid across the figure,
now, with a tortoise-shell comb
appeared piled high,
and bodice again in place.

At the garret window she started—
spun away the needle, thread looping back and falling
behind the glass rose
as though appliqued in silk
and sucking in all the sky's blue
high waters:

water, water
all around—
everywhere,
gurgling, creeping
choking water. And just then
he, going off without having looked about,
had waded
along the stairs into the rifted flood
river.

   Inara Cedrins

DON JUAN AND DOÑA

   1
Like a spider's weaving
her muslin dress
was blown into a whirlpool
about her thighs, tightened around the middle,
embracing kneecaps and with them the snapdragons

that rose to her knees,
                    and really—
her skin had a gentleness of snapdragons
but the wind, not a lover, with no restraint
embraced it.

   2
You, on whose muslin dress printed fish
moon-imprisoned, flutter over yellow irises—
throw down
and show up this pale imitation garden's brilliance;
it's not after an angel's pattern those two clay
oranges in place of breasts
are, but two southern suns, heated blood
in glowing flesh!

   3
Your dresses' fish and irises
will lose color,
                    in your eyes
dimness settle, and the light flee from your hair;
among pale irises you'll walk, pale yourself,
when the compactness of fruit has left your shape.
In your breasts
yet like a shy lark some leaping
but sent-for joy
without sin
an angel will die.

   4
Without hesitation, without the slightest hurry
without passion
carelessly
they parted.
                    And the secret (not
deep,
but a covert joy)
went out before him into night's extinguished streets,

hiding its beginning within itself
and its end.

     5

That vision of yours will pale, oh Don Juan,
from the furtively left mansion's
sleeping chambers!
                    Quenching
gentle memories from the beloved's eyes, time
covers all as swiftly as the wind blowing dust
abandoned by your boots on the threshing-floor.

Soon proffered to a new lover
like a white mathiola she'll bear herself,
from your lips of cinnamon all
scented still, but you
no longer in the memory of that fine lady.

  Inara Cedrins

SOVIET LATVIAN POETS

VIZMA BELŠEVICA   1931–

Vizma Belševica is among the most popular poets in Soviet Latvia. She attended the Latvian State University in Riga and the Gorki Institute of Literature in Moscow. At the institute she met Bella Akhmadulina, Yuri Kazakov, and Andrei Voznesenski, who have praised her as an outstanding Soviet poet. A heart ailment and official reprobation have forced her to suspend her creative work. She has published five volumes of poetry and a book of short stories. Belševica's work has been translated into more than a dozen languages, and she has made recordings of her own poetry. She also has written film scripts and translated works by Russian, British, and American authors into Latvian.

SALOME

If I didn't take your head,
you'd take mine.
Only at executioner's axe would you lose daring.

My eyes,
burnt while lost in the black light of your hair,
would gaze lifelessly into your face.

My cheeks,
fallen in through nights of waiting and despair,
would freeze in lines of bitterness.

But the kisses that sought your mouth
would break through the tense fabric of lips

and pour as heated blood
into the silver bowl of your disdain,
Jokanaan.

Inara Cedrins

SNAIL IN INVERTED GOBLET

Snail in the inverted goblet of mushroom cap,
bee seeking shelter in poppy—
beloved, to what rains
are your eyes shut?

Under rosy streaming roofs
frail stigmas of convolvulus—
beloved, to what a night
have you left me out?

To a grey night of rain.
And that blueness shivering in the distance—
that's phosphor in rotten wood,
that's not morning.

Inara Cedrins

THERE IN THAT WHIRLPOOL

There, in that deep whirlpool,
the maple has probably drowned—
only two spread palms
circle silently over the black depths.
An autumn water-nymph she'll become
and lure us into leafy billows
and all the ghost-month October
we'll have to roam garden to garden.
We'll pass as though bewitched

through autumn toward winter,
still searching, still not believing
that the most beautiful has drowned . . .

Inara Cedrins

DON'T GO, WOMEN

Don't go, women!
                    Don't go to the sea
to scoop up sand in low shoes . . .
Listen to me, women, stay on the corner
where through rings of light loops the linden's gold.

In the rippling of fall leaves, in gaudy fence slats,
words have somewhere to go, eyes have someplace to flee . . .
There, beyond the mute dunes, if someone looks in one's face,
the heart can't hide in the shore's sparseness.

Line of white froth. The vertical stone wall of dark.
Only one reply can be thrown to the silence.
Guard yourselves, women!
                    I once went to the sea.
She who came back, was no longer I.

Inara Cedrins

THE MAPLE BLOSSOM

Like a thin maple seed in your breast pocket
Among the day's grit, you don't even notice,
You forget, you don't know, that with you,
In each step, in each thought, you are carrying me,
That the dampness of the moment—tears or a kiss—

Will make a tree burst out from the fine seed—
A tree so fierce that hearts will be ravaged
With the agony of taking root and of blossoming.

Juris Rozītis

PAINTING SIGNATURES

1
Botticelli's "Aphrodite's Birth"

Yes, of course, you're of the sea's froth, of the blaze
that glides over the waves' clearness,
of a split pearl-oyster's rosy glimmer,
of cloud reflections, Aphrodite.

I—only of earth. Heavy as clay;
but heaviness can sprout a most intoxicating shoot,
and in airy tufts of hops
one can become dizzied to unconsciousness, Aphrodite.

What depth sinks deeper than lilac in bloom?
One falls more heatedly into hayrick than whirlpool.
While only earth can quench a thirsting seed
I do not fear you, Aphrodite.

Let man sacrifice a dove to you . . . in the white wing
a red drop of earthly blood shines.
Who is born of woman, will return
again to woman, Aphrodite.

2
Goya's "Saturn Devouring His Children"

My most unfortunate man with your son's blood on your lips,
with ferocious famine, that eats at your insides . . .
What do you feel when our bones crunch,

you hear them, between your teeth?
When your fingers break
our ribs?
When you see naked heart
steaming in your palm?
Do your somber eyes divine
that your sons pity you?
We tended our herds,
we sowed grain, that your tables might break
under the loaf's weight.
On the sparse cliff's rock
we nursed grapevines, that wine might flow
over your thirsts.
Together with sons
you'd forget famine, if you didn't kill us.
But the cows' udders swell up with milky fullness.
There're no milkers. Oxen wander without a shepherd.
There's no reaper—kernels grow beards in the ears
and fruit overripened without a taker bursts.
Already my blood rains down your chin . . .
Father, what will you do, when you run out of sons?

3
Rossetti's "Beatrice and Dante in Paradise"

Did you exist, Beatrice?
You did not.
The monument's stone lies of your birth and death.
You never were.
Tall columns of light fell through brilliant window apertures.
Distant skies in your eyes—a play of light.
So you were born.
Your mother—a streak of blue glass.
Father—Dante's glance.
You died, when the hot sheaf of the sun was painfully extinguished.
Beatrice, Beatrice,

Florentine Philistine in a churchgoing throng . . .
He knew this with his mind, great Dante.
Heart believing in miracles and beating in sharp verse.
To love for a lifetime the nonexistent—circles of hell.
To love the extinguished ray,
Beatrice, what torture . . .
Paradise—only lies,
binding flesh to life.
Everyone mentions Dante's Hell,
but no one speaks of his Paradise.

Inara Cedrins and Astrida Stahnke

DON'T BE OVERSURE

Don't be oversure of your cherry tree.
Don't speak of roots. Of the fact that it's planted.
You see: in the vibrating wings of thrushes
a tree opens out branches. Berries tremble piercingly.
Birds don't call there. Leaves applaud
that easterner, who lifts the cherry in air.
And don't shake your head and say no,
the skies aren't a great Cherry Way,
but earth . . . the earth too will not say
against what it presses its grizzled nettles.
From green clouds a red rain falls.
You've a cherry in your garden? Don't be so sure.

Inara Cedrins

THAT WAS A POLITE FISH

That was a very polite fish . . .
when we were entangled in the sun-rays' net
which swung under the sharp wave edges,

the fish said: Glad to become acquainted
with a cold-blooded sister! How becoming to you
this blueness of face . . .
            I replied: Fish,
if I were blood sister to you
we'd not meet.
            It was hurt
and turned tail to me.
            Take no offense . . .
I lie deep at the bottom of a forest
and above, spruces are green at wave crests,
striking up cloud froth occasionally in the wind.

   Inara Cedrins

THAT WOMAN . . .

That woman is sleepwalking. Don't call!
Past what a chorus of looks, going with outstretched hand,
to what a smile. But you can't wait.
You call. That woman yet again falls upon stones
and yet for what uncounted time rises. She doesn't leave
                                    herself there.
She takes her stance by the laundry. Lights the gas fire.
Tends flowers on windowsills. In the broken bones pains
but one eternal longing—to climb to that gable-end.
The somnambulist waits for night and mixes the batter
                                    for pancakes.
Not for the sake of the moon. Just because
at night it's more rare for someone to call.

   Inara Cedrins

I WON'T KNOCK

I won't knock at your door,
won't turn toward the light in your window,
will take up buckets. Lift yoke to shoulders.
The well's deepness will reflect clear in the night.

Glittering midnight to the brim,
I'll draw up and carry to the house.
I'll sit down in the same place at the end of the bench,
forgetting, for what reason I went after water.

What did I go for? The heaviness of yoke to shoulders
was necessary? For it wasn't water I thirsted for.
Nor for you. Listen how the sea wind slumps
against the calm dune.

Speechlessness remains. An odd gentleness remains—
it neither wants anything, nor asks anything.
The blossom grows still and turns it cheek to night.
In quiet droplets dew falls out.

Inara Cedrins

THE AUTUMN COBWEB

The autumn cobweb of dew
pearly silver—
like tears of happiness
when the heart's already wise

and doesn't ask more
than the white moment

before the droplets slide down
along the sun's shears

and again dry
burns in Indian Summer
that juniper glade
whose greenness is past.

Inara Cedrins

THE CHESTNUT TREE

A chestnut tree walks down the street in full bloom . . .
His branches touch a window pane. It breaks.
The room fills with the drone of furious bees.

A chestnut tree walks down the street in full bloom . . .
Wherever its whiteness dawns, the greyness
Of familiar coziness sets. Traffic stops.

A chestnut tree walks down the street in full bloom,
And people don't know what to do, what to be.
And the lowliest person feels lower still,

When the chestnut tree goes by in full bloom
Bumping against window sills with foaming jugs.
He's drunk again—what else?

A chestnut tree walks down the street in full bloom—
So exceedingly large, so exceedingly beautiful
That the chestnut should be kept off the streets.

Juris Rozītis

NIGHT INDENTATIONS

The boys are asleep. Keds sleep in the hallway. In the kitchen
blue potatoes lie under a towel.
Upon the shoulder of lemon peel, a pilchard head
lies in the trash can. Hollow
in the shaft the elevator sleeps and won't choke the breath
clanging doors at our floor. The telephone
lies in white sleep alongside a glove with a hole in it
and will not cry out. Tired flesh
sleeps open-eyed and allows itself to be carried
toward morning by darkness—flash—darkness—
against the wall . . .
      (indentation about a blank stanza)
      . . . hear me white wall, blank stanza:
      upon you the faint shadow of a naked branch
      is free to wind writing. Each thought's bud
      so clearly sketched. (Still the old leaf
      shivers on the stem, next to the bud that's ready.
      From the tender folds to new shoots
      everything's in there. Flower too.) Of anxiety,
      overtired, sleepless as roots
      the tiniest threads of ravaging life
      swell with pulsating sap—to feed, open
      those winter buds and against white wall
      peer through lashes and ascertain
      with the alert unmistakenness of conscience, who's awake.
. . . for the soul isn't asleep and won't allow flesh to sleep.
Through Old Riga it roams for countless nights now,
exchanging glances with cats' glittering eyes,
for cats too don't sleep—they have to watch
where the soul goes—and cats see.
The free ones see, who, in dark gateways,
sit like jugs or pad the damp cobblestones
with sickening paws. And those locked in,
with eyes that shine behind windows of black glass
like golden coins, which an obsessed miser
hides in a purse in the dark. Yes, and the mist sees,

for the mist too does not sleep. Grey muteness
feels around rings of light and shadow fragments
as though searching for words, but finds nothing,
only a soul which also searches for words
or the echo of steps. And the cats watch
how it walks—like a child with grey hair.
    (indentation about the grey-haired child)
    the child awoke and saw it was grey-haired
    but didn't understand the mirror—only blew breath
    onto the grey places, with a hand
    rubbed them, and, skipping as usual,
    frolicked down the stairs—to others.
    But others addressed it formally: Aunt:
    and bent knees in a curtsey, and boys
    scraped a foot and crossed
    over to the end of the yard, and silence
    like an unacknowledged greeting spread over the path.
    The child followed. Friends retreated
    like the sky's edge. Lips quivered.
    The child wanted to cry and saw it couldn't,
    and began to understand.
    Merciful midnight.
Toward day's unreachable horizons
it curls fingers of mist like a warm palm
about Riga's sleep. Green towers sleep through
the piercing upward thrust in that grey palm,
and in the lap of each tower—a copper bell.
The child approaches, blows on it with its breath—the circle of breath
remains for an instant on the bell's cheek
and trickles together into a mute tear. That is the bell
or the child! With tongue tied back
to the crossbeam with a damp-swollen rope!
And words, words for the bell's loneliness,
where are those words! Riga's roofs unfold,
scaly wings patched with tin
over sleeping lives. Through electric wires
and the sinuous paths of light—downward,

listening at each window, side by side in breathing
yet each in itself contained. Strange dreams flutter
past the child's eyes—all self contained. To take
by the hands—all together—as in that tale
where they'd be loved to this very day
if not dead—but hands pull away
from the child's fingers. Part. The child remains,
having searched in vain for the connecting word
with its dolls and marbles.

       (indentation about dolls and marbles)
       Not to create again, but to collect and collect, and collect
       with grey-haired solicitousness for fear of want,
       and where to get them! Be it the garden's corner,
       where other maples burned and it was nothing—
       but one, crazed, really did burn down;
       or an organ, not the Cathedral's, the ruddy pipes
       of tiny streets, where the wind plays with sand
       and adolescents lean on the pedals—to death
       in that roar and catch of breath
       unaware . . . and I didn't notice
       that step across the boundary of love
       and out! Free! A fraction above earth,
       without you and not thinking of you,
       with eyes open, that you don't impede
       against the eternity of faces and lips quivering
       like mute seaweed in a brown current,
       with open heart—taking seaweed along
       and, saying the word, going over for long
       those dolls of mine, those marbles of mine,
       against that smooth wall when darkness—flash—darkness
       and in darkness the word.
Night floats toward morning. Floats tired and tiring.
Still able to motate. Your duty sleeps.
The boys sleep. Keds sleep in the hallway. In the kitchen
under a towel, blue . . . yes, and flesh sleeps,
which one time a child will approach
with Riga's mist in its hair. Long it will gaze

at the stout woman, whose forehead even in sleep
is furrowed, and her hands swollen.
The child will draw back—afraid of the strange lady.
And won't return. With the bell's tear
will rise against azure on the dim ribbon of vapor
and evaporate. The tiniest indentation.
And nothing further. Only sunrise over Riga.
And the ships' hollow parting whistle from the harbor
sallying out into immeasurably distant seas.

Inara Cedrins

WORDS ABOUT WORDS

                        Words came in dream. Words
                        stood about me like boys
                        who through their mother's fault
                        are called to the militia. The smallest,
                        most lovable, word's rounded mouth
                        became angular and
                        quivered. It seemed he would all at once
                        scream: I won't do it
                        any more! But in vain. He wasn't
                        a screaming word. And then I
                        said:

Words, my words—when we are again judged,
don't hang your heads. The dock of the accused
is only a track worn thin, that must be stepped over, to begin
a world without walls. An earth, not a room.
Once in a lifetime everyone has to hatch from the egg.
Birds are aware of this. Everyone is. Everyone. Even the hen.
It's known to the bird. Poet and word.
Judgment, even the highest judgment—that's freedom,
which can no longer be taken away. Who is touched by the
                                                outside breath

doesn't need to look back on his walls—life.
Birds die, and poets. But not even the axe's edge
can hack out the word that is said before death.
The words, once poured out, can not be bailed up by anyone.
Like swallows in the skies no one can pen them.
Words, my words, do not pity me!
The grain must not pity the field, from which the ear grows.
Without shoots and without ploughshares the earth quickly withers.
Cleave more deeply, with more pain—to a new thought's budding.

It's not your sorrow: glory or punishment.
Finishing the poem, gates close between us.
Go further alone. In giving you life
I answer for everything, words, my words . . .

   Inara Cedrins

IN FEAR

In fear of the moment
when it will no longer be possible not to see the truth
I cover my eyes with a chestnut flower
which you once gave to me,
I press my ears shut with the small birds
which once wound themselves over us,
I cover my heart with those mild evenings the two of us spent
by a purplish blue sea
and hang on to the fading ribbon of sunset at the edge of the sky
in fear of the moment
when it will no longer be possible not to see the truth.

   Juris Rozītis

MĀRIS ČAKLAIS   1940-

Māris Čaklais lives in Riga, and he has published ten volumes of poetry since 1965. Čaklais has been active as an essayist, novelist, and transla-tor, as well as a promoter of culture who makes frequent appearances before rural audiences. He has made recordings of his poetry and ac-cepted editorial assignments with Literatūra un Māksla (Literature and the Arts), the most authoritative Soviet Latvian publication in its field. Čaklais has traveled abroad and has visited the United States.

SETTING CHESTNUT TREES ALIGHT

While the mind was asleep
quietly and with light foot
someone tonight has gone
and set afire the chestnut trees.

What phosphor, no, in what pain,
into what sorrow do you dip,
so that in the pre-dawn rich darkness
fingers blossom like candles?

A woman passes. Fire nears
one yet waiting candle.
How many long to be kindled!
How many there are, who fear it!

How to measure the voltage
in the charged air?
How to grasp the moment
when buds open themselves up?

   Inara Cedrins

WOMAN IN MOURNING

Unobtrusive, with deep eyes, distant,
she came in like a black seaweed.

Conversation froze on the spot.
Eyelids lowered like wings.

For a year now her son—a ghost
draws watercolors in heaven's garden.

What can one say—to the woman in black?
A word, before taking substance, turns to ash.

What has she to do—with us, who are alive?
Each one living in unwilling tearer open of wound.

Silence like a spider wove its web.
In the field trees drew on black garb.

Sadness, what did you want? What was it?
You sent no stand-in this time, revealed yourself . . .

   Inara Cedrins

OVERGROWN LAKE

   . . . I'll make love to you. The beginning of my love
                                 will be timid, but weaving
   like seagrasses, like seadistance, like a nest of
                                 woven reeds,

I'll kiss the slimy stomachs of boats and the hands
                              reaching for waterlilies,
a covey of ducklings will rise in a group, blue feathers flashing
                              in a lightray, reed-mace
                              will bloom once more,
and I'll love you more and more passionately, and more inclusive
                              each instant
of lithe swimmers, washers and waders, beetles, crawlers, fliers,
                  I'll love you all in your entirety
with your entrails, insects, ducks, sunken
                              cities and sirens,
water spirits and dragonflies that, cognizant, rise
                  over
my love, but soon turn back, circling in the open
waters' surface, which I leave to your freedom,
                              you need it so,
not to feel the tight circle of reeds, which slowly
                  without a shadow arrives unseen
so that in your sweet-blind subsiding you settle in love's
                              strangling circlet.

Inara Cedrins

JULY NIGHT

This warm, good night
plucks you like a flower
and ruminates long, long.
How warm such lips are,
how gentle such sandpaper!
Night eats you quietly,
and it's strange that it doesn't hurt;
that must be because it's so slowly,
little by little.
Oh, into such a moist mouth
one can enter without looking back!

Night eats you quietly,
night chafes you white,
night grinds you sharp;
no, that's no angel wing
nor hand, but the scythe—
I call no one
along with me into night's meadows
but, if you like, come . . .

   Inara Cedrins

CHILD

   1
He's of your flesh, from your flesh, already off,
inexorably floating away like a boat, drawing distant,
through milky fog, waving through the mists of hope with a hand.

The waves comfort you, till evening's blaze
floods over you, and in its clarity you see
that you yourselves are in the boat, that he remains on shore.

You greet the shore, you yourselves were once the shore.

   2
But now you're waves among waves
hoping that once in the incessant stream there'll be
the hand of one current, familiarly warm.

Then, winged—in surprise—from the heights
you'll rise with the sun and wind in affinity
to pour out over earth, sown field and grass.

His returning is your return.

   Inara Cedrins

106   Māris Čaklais

GIVE ME YOUR KNIFE

. . . give me your silver knife, right here
is that midnight tree (oh, grass,
how blackgreen you are in the moon's zenith!)—
let's peel the nightfruit together;
oh, if you haven't a silver knife, give
if only nail file, see
how blue the dew is on the skin;
oh, if you haven't, oh, if I have nothing else,
let's enter the midnight fruit with our lips;
with lips, with teeth, with fingers, with illusions
(somewhere beyond the hills shines hope's pale-blue razors edge)
let's split it open and spill out, spill out
every last thing, that we can possibly spill, and, fully
satiated and sticking to one another, let's awaken
when lackluster sleep is split by morning's spontaneous generation.

   Inara Cedrins

DEDICATION

Seven years the boar's ham is drying,
Seven years pain glowers with sheathed nails.
Life alone as bread—wind on the exposed table,
Measuring only once, cutting seven times.

But for millions of years the moon silvers fish,
For a million years the boar and pain circle.
Tear off a piece of ham, pain will tear it from you,
Let's toss this life a kopeck—for we do want to return.

   Inara Cedrins

DECEMBER SKY

Not the smallest ray
is left of that radiance.
Calm and strong is the weave of the dark.
Merely imagined, the fondling touch of a branch
and somebody's weeping among the raspberry canes.

No one is weeping.
Spent, over-spent, are all tears.
And, when one considers, why should one have wept—
springtimes are sure to be steaming like kettles
and autumn will settle the whole of the bill.

I also shall pay.
At present, left in abeyance.
There simply is nowhere to turn, to catch hold of the moment
that holds out salvation. The pharmacy's door stands closed.
Through heavy shutters, some light makes its way.

Underfoot, a chestnut
down in the mud, driven in.
But even in darkness I feel that it celebrates.
Light is wintering in each single thing
even if no one is there to awaken it.

Ruth Speirs

WINTER IN COURLAND

Beyond the dark pine forests
among rabbit and deer trails
stand houses with blue windows
and an apple orchard beside each.

Trees creak and bend in a blizzard . . .
But when the whistling wind dies down

108   Māris Čaklais

a child's quivering breath
melts a circle on the icy windowpane.

One person's curiosity
watches the shadows thicken.
The desires of the little one
fall asleep like the day—slowly.

He doesn't feel the veined hands
that lift him and put him to bed,
how the runners behind the window squeak
and men come by with heavy tread,

how the weary horses breathe,
how their breath rises to the skies,
there, where the stars begin glittering
in an unknown vastness.

Fire speaks warmly and quietly
with a tongue like a shaving, so light.
The little one is deep in sleep,
just as the world is, in snow.

   Inara Cedrins

STRANGE EVENINGS

Those are strange evenings. Cows
come back from grazing with heavy udders.
Apples fall into the grass. Carts of grain
sway into the courtyards.

These evenings in accouchement rooms
warm mouths don't cry out from pain.
These evenings clarity arrives
and the tortured "why?" subsides.

In door frames, as in photographs,
mothers glimpse their shot-down sons.

Those are strange evenings. In them
nothing comes too late.

Evening again. But what star is that,
that slides humming toward earth?
That's not a star. There at the airfield returns
Captain Saint-Exupery.

Inara Cedrins

A WOMAN CALLS

A woman calls a black bird into her yard,
feeds it with tears and moist rye grains;
and the bird gobbles up the brown grain seeking green shoots
and asks for more . . .

You have much more to give.
But beware of giving all to despair—
take one handful to sow over the cool earth
and wait—before the blue dawn it'll sprout.

Then the bird will come again. And seek the green shoots.
But then beneath each eyelid a raven will perch,
upon each wing a sharp sun.
No, feed your grains confidently to the bird!

Inara Cedrins

BUTTERFLY CEMETERY

When you die, butterfly,
along the abandoned field path,
I'll solicit autumn's trumpet
to accompany you to the spirits;

as funeral train, we'll yoke birches
in trappings woven by spiders;

plucking the last somber grasses
cows will accompany us,

the bee will fly yet another late
fearful, weaving circle,
the aspen will lay on the grave
its veined, trembling hand . . .

The trumpet, your lonely march—
let it not be overlong,
your life itself was not long,
your freedom did not last long
(only such a butterfly freedom,
only such a butterfly life) . . .

No,
copper doesn't resound in you,
therefore
through somber gates of mountain ash
let sound your lonely march—
                    trumpet!

Elephants, blue-grey and mighty,
rest in marked jungle cemeteries.
The butterfly's transparent wings
are superimposed on earth's autumn.

   Inara Cedrins

THE GIRL IN WHITE

In a white camisole straight out of winter—of a snowdrift!
But over it gushes a river of cherry and apple trees . . .

Not a leaf—only a mad blossoming.
Not a word—only the sounding icicle of silence.

Scattering on the white beret, the white boots wade
on earth white with the chill of blossoms—

and closer, and closer. This dance! This fire! I extinguish.
Girl, snowflake, don't come nearer, I'll melt you!

Remain white! For—other summers belong to me.
I, good icicle, don't wish to see, don't wish your tears.

Inara Cedrins

LIFE

In the window,
fire maiden.
In the oven—
warm bread.

Fire and bread,
child, in your language—
that is my homeland
on a May morning.

> 'I draw all pain
> through a thornbush,
> through a burred bush;
> I draw all pain
> through stone.'

And become rich as bread.
And become clean as fire.
And become pliant as language.

Inara Cedrins

DOLCE MARIA

1
In silver shoes
over the silver sea
come, Dolce Maria,

come half-dream,
come half-waking
reminding me of your existence.
The ocean tonight
will thrum at your feet:
Dolce Maria—
Sweet Maria . . .
Over the black depths
on water skiis
such a moment flees—
ungovernable.
　　Ungovernable. Ungraspable.
　　Not to be struck down with lightning.
In silver shoes
over the silver sea,
yellow suns as earrings—
maiden?
moment?
apparition
that disappears, never
to turn back?
No, to return.
But perhaps—
only the moon's bridge
over the sleeping sea?

　2
. . . sleeping . . .
　　Is the sea asleep?
. . . the sun flooded toward me, sudden sun, sprinkling, pouring,
filling full the mouth, eyes and ears like sleep, fish disturbed
began darting (perhaps not fish, but happiness?), comprehending
that swimming was now necessary, late, but comprehending and
as though slipping free of seaweed—brushed off prejudices,
presumptions and still other slimy "pre's".
　　But during the night mist descended, ships began lowing,
and of this lowing the sea awoke, and a whale with its tail
churned up clouds to the stars, and the stars swung like buoys

Māris Čaklais　113

upward, downward, and seemed to cry: "At least with eyes
hold fast to the stars!".

Two seas, two, and alive, and both—a moment
like a stone thrown into a whirlpool casts circles, and these
vibrate like the rings of years . . .

3

Let's drink to the burial,
let's drink to the burial, Dolce Maria,
to the instant in which
you were no longer
only the company's MELIA representative,
let's drink to the burial of that instant, which
was joyfully born before our eyes,
and let's go
gloss over Europe.

Let's gloss over
all those other
continents too, let's take
of each
one shiny postcard,
let's wash
the spat-upon streets as though a shameful word
with scented children's
soap.

Let's view parades,
villas and barracks
well ordered.

In the glitter of weapons
faces like thin milk-skin
will become ashen,
but the cockades'
coppery gleam
will lift upward
the mortal souls.

4

Black as blackbirds
with white cravats
(as in Riga or Kuldiga)
the Catholic school children skip.

Then perhaps
nevertheless
that moment
hasn't died,
Dolce Maria?
But duty
remains duty,

you continue fulfilling
duty:

5

"In this church Columbus prayed to God,
before he went forth to discover America."

Oh, good Columbus,
oh, dear God . . .

And America was discovered
through both . . .

But what will you advise us,
Dolce Maria?
Where shall we
lay our little kneelers,
so it's softer to the knees—
in prayer?

Where do we pray to our God,
we twentieth century unbelieving
believers?

But perhaps—it wasn't even worth
discovering that America?

For "John Brown's buried . . .

. . . .

(and a great silence in the middle,
so it's possible to count all those
who were killed)

. . . .

in his conquering path . . ."

6

But you in your turn
on the road of your victory,
you,
standing at the outposts of paradise
(and the Canary Islands can really be called
paradise's antechamber:

       cooked canarybirds sing
       freely in locked cages),

and so you,
standing at the outposts of paradise,
lying, sitting, eating,
why have your eyes
a sadness
like dogs'?
Why is your sleep
so feverish
and your wakefulness—the same?
"We were happy
in our caves,"
the people say, transferred
to glass and concrete cages.

"Perhaps actually,"
you said, Dolce Maria,
"we'd be happy again,
if we returned to caves?"

And consequently—
a solution?

7
Dolce Maria,
in the moment when the sudden
sun floods back,
in Algiers
the casbah awakens.

Every rich mother's daughter
drives a limousine,
every rich son
looks over with a smirk,

but through thirty-year-old
watery trachoma eyes
the indigent quarter
stares at the world.

Average life expectancy—
thirty,
thirty-five.
But their achievements still exist,
still their joys—
of eight children
half are healthy,
and yesterday it was possible
to buy sausage . . .

And this would be
a solution?

8
Each land is so preoccupied
with its casbah,
that it has no time
to recognize that moment
when in the first belch of satiety
intrudes a taste of wormwood—
calcification
of nerve grooves in the brain.

9

Upward, downward, and to remain in place—such is the buoy
and the stars' destiny in storm.
                              Upward, downward, and—only
forward: such is a person's destiny in journeying.
                                        Two seas,
two, and alive, and both—a moment as when
stone tossed into whirlpool casts circles, and the rings
                                        of years vibrate . . .

10

Not "dolce vita"
not "c'est la vie",
not "oh my God!",
will save the world.
Peace, that comes after
prodding unrest.
God, who wavers
in the eyes of unbelievers.
Wakefulness, that holds
bird in flight.
Humanity, that turns aside
buckshot from the elk.

11

In silver shoes
over the silver sea—
how warm it still is
in the moon's light . . .
And the moon's bridge
over the glittering sea,
how it yet is
a stable bridge.
In silver shoes

you go away
with yellow suns in your earrings . . .

Sun bursts its eggshell.
The shark emerges.
Day awakens.

Inara Cedrins

ĀRIJA ELKSNE   1928–

Ārija Elksne (pseudonym of Demidova) is not a prolific poet, but she enjoys a popularity in Soviet Latvia for her lyrical poetry that celebrates family life and the beauties of the land. She is also much praised for her children's poetry. Elksne has made several recordings of her work, and she is active as a translator and as an editor of literary publications.

EVENING

Like a destitute painter, evening
    brings your portrait to me
And, having placed it in a frame of darkness,
    hangs it up in the scarlet maple . . .
I say to him angrily
    that I've no desire to see such,
And if he doesn't know how to draw anything else
    then it'd be best not to exhibit . . .
But evening, as though rooted to earth,
    remains standing at the window,
And, closing my eyes, I feel
    your portrait dimming on the maple branch . . .

    Inara Cedrins

A COUPLE OF CENTURIES FROM NOW

White house among dark-green trees,
and lilac blooms by the porch . . .
Any moment now Tatyana will come to the window,
any moment now Olga will sunnily begin smiling . . .

Any moment now there'll be exhaled the scent of lavender,
a soft rustle of pale crimson silk;
the strange, untouched taste of youth
coming unnoticed along with all this.

. . . Escalators, machines, haste and stress
will still exist a couple of centuries from now;
much will these years bring to us, women,
much will have to be left in the past—

There, where the white house stands among trees,
there, where pale crimson silk rustles softly;
where, over Tatyana's quivering hand
shines a candle in a silver sconce.

   Inara Cedrins

WITH A FROZEN FACE

Soon trees will toss leaves to the ground,
soon an icy cover will harden over the stream,
and my journey to Japan, to the sun land,
probably won't come through . . .
I take chrysanthemums on my lap
and reckon in my head: how many
there are, who don't love me
and won't be indebted to me

because, with a frozen face
I go past their smiles.

   Inara Cedrins

AND AFTERWARD

What happens, when the fairy tale ends,
when all the wedding guests drive off?—
And Cinderella remains
and doesn't know quite what to do with the crown.

And the court attendants begin sneering,
and the prince draws his brows together threateningly,
and Cinderella sits crying
in the palace park, under a jasmine bush.

And banquets are held again—
and the prince drinks without moderation,
and at last four men
carry him away from the table.

Then, having seen clearly for a while
that everyone thinks only of the prince,
Cinderella runs away
and in her haste loses a slipper.

But the prince doesn't demand for a second time
to search every path . . .
No, fairy tales, friends, aren't lies:
it's just that they don't tell everything.

   Inara Cedrins

FEMININITY

   *"You aren't feminine,
   You were never helpless."*
                              —my daughter

No, woman, your real name is not frailty,
your name is not helplessness—
that's only seeming, only playful progress

as if a phosphorescent lighting up . . .
Beyond veils, beyond powder, beyond ringlets,
beyond shoulders enticingly bare
your strength is hoarded at the very center of the heart
and never turns to ash.
Long ago the floods of war would have washed
my people from earth
if you had given weakness space in yourself,
if you had let pain free.
Who knows if humanity would ever have arrived
at our century
if your hands had stopped giving and supporting,
if your lips had said "difficult."
No, woman, your real name is not frailty,
your name is not helplessness,
you are sanctuary and invitation open to the sun.
And desire to live.

Inara Cedrins

LIKE A STEPDAUGHTER

Day came so unwillingly,
breaking through thickets of darkness
and weeping in drops of rain,
wailing with soughing winds . . .

like a stepdaughter, whose new mother
gives her to a man impossible to love,
without a single good word
shoving her out the door . . .

And involuntarily the breast heaves
and involuntarily the pulse races
and, comforted by apathy,
the dull knife cuts through bread.

Oh, time of being cheated and abandoned,
when words are broken and lying begins,
when, in clothing soaked with darkness,
day comes so unwillingly!

Inara Cedrins

WE PRETENDED

We pretended not to notice, when the moment,
when the strangeness arrived—came and passed;
perhaps we'd missed only a second,
but now the moment had grown to a ravine.
And I now know it'll be like this for lifetimes;
we'll note the distance and the measure—
no, no, I'm not unhappy, I don't sigh,
I swear to notice these occurrences.
I'm learning to rejoice over the aroma
of your voice thrown across distances;
when at the side of the window covered by ice flowers
a threatening and bitter frost roams
and the time stands at my door, when
one must speak of oneself more easily, more
$\qquad\qquad\qquad\qquad\qquad\qquad$ imperceptibly.

Inara Cedrins

THE CHILD OF THE ATOMIC AGE

The child of the atomic age lies down
among rockets, tanks and land mines,
the child of the atomic age lies
and wonders at a blossom.
Itself still as velvety as a catkin,
fingers rosy and tiny,

124   Ārija Elksne

and, as in distant prehistoric times—
as helpless.
The child of the atomic age lies down
and in its wide eyes
the blue skies of summer
look with trust.
Looking just the same
as when among cloud puffs
children saw only
birds, birds, more birds.
Mother sits by the child—
contemporary and wise,
the mother sits in the shadow of arms
and feels like an ant.

   Inara Cedrins

REGRET

Regret these obstacles
through which we arrive back at our roots—
at the beginning of all good things,
at that of which orchids spring
and bend toward us their idle faces—
not butterflies nor flowers, but something odd,
difficult to express in our tongue;
for in Latvia meadowsweet and mare's tail grow
and the master potter fixes handles to clay cups—
but orchids come from somewhere deep in jungles
and sometimes grow—so simply—upon limbs.
Regret these obstacles!
Through what words, through what stupid jokes!

   Inara Cedrins

DOWRY

And when the morning of my wedding dawned beyond the window
my mother gave me linen sheets to add to my dowry.

Let my life flow toward autumn
peacefully and smoothly.

What will I give to my daughter?

I'll give her unrest, which is breathed into the storm by the sea,
so that the peace of a calm autumn day is forever stranger to it.

   Inara Cedrins

APPLE YEAR

It's rough to be an apple in an apple year;
prices are low and there's a huge selection,
you're passed up and not even glanced at,
undesired and unpraised . . .
To hang to the branch with one's last strength?
One can do it—but what's the point?
Even so, to the next autumn
you won't hold yourself, you won't save yourself . . .
You'll be ground up and pressed into juice,
this year—take note—is an apple year!
And that juice—it'll be taken and drunk down,
without anyone sensing just what you were.

   Inara Cedrins

THE DEMON

(to Eduard Kanavs)

Night moves. I hear the whir of wings.
He's flying here. He wants to drink my heart.
Like Tamara, he draws and calls me,
confusing my head with sweet promises . . .
He sings. And the sounds are sucked in by every weave.
And one wants to fall to one's knees and weep, weep, weep . . .

Oh, beloved, don't be harsh toward me,
only your goodness is my guard!
If you turn away and he flies to me again,
I can't answer then . . .
              Then go find yourself another.

   Inara Cedrins

ONLY WITH FOOD

Only with food, only with drink
we're called a gathering, tied together;
only with songs sung by forbears
is the soul lifted slightly over the table.
Each with a piece of ice in the breast,
each with artificial honey upon tongue . . .
Wanting to relinquish—but with unsure hands;
wanting to lean back—but no broad shoulder in reach.
Only with food, only with drink
we're called a gathering, tied together—
give, Fortune, one communal ache,
to lift us winged, purifying us.

   Inara Cedrins

THE GRASSHOPPER'S VIOLIN

The grasshopper's sad violin
hangs from a grey spear grass;
migrating birds with wings spread
touch the desire to leave.
Gladiolus and asters
are dishes for the parting feast,
dinosaur combines
have eaten of the grainfields.
Heart so swollen,
so sorrowful without reason;
a buoy of blueblack cloud
cleaved by scissors of rays—
autumn.

Inara Cedrins

LILAC BLOOMS IN ITS OWN TIME

I've stepped aside a little now
from life's seething turmoil,
to where mathiolas breathe about me
and evening stands beyond the gates, blue and quiet,
to where women await men home from work
holding their fortune in their hands,
to where feelings become calm and pure—
like a glowing coal that kindles the hearth,
where children are raised and it's believed there'll be no
extinguishing of the flames of Earth in a tight stovepipe,
where at times one sighs and weeps in secret
if some fine thorn at times punctures the heart . . .

Inara Cedrins

OJĀRS VĀCIETIS   1933–1983

*Ojārs Vācietis enjoyed popularity in Soviet Latvia as "the Latvian Yev-
tushenko." He was a prolific writer, with several volumes of poetry to
his credit. Vācietis was well known also for his activities as translator,
literary critic, and editor. His poetry has been translated in more than
thirty languages. In 1982 he was awarded the USSR State Prize for
poetry.*

BURNING LEAVES

"Manuscripts don't burn."

  M. Bulgakov

What a musical score under the chestnut!
What fingers!

What novels
under the old linden!

What odes about the light
under the oak chandelier!

What tiny, spark-like poem children
under the birch!

And they'll burn. And—ashes. And you, old woman, having gotten
  free

of this rather messy work, you haven't gotten free. Only to you
it's like another year past in your life, but in eternity, honored,
not only years don't disappear, but micron bits of minutes. I have to
    inform you
dear, that, when spring is burned, or summer, fall—that that is hap-
    pening already
in the next spring—and this one in the next; and I stand embalmed
in this smoke of yours, and you are a sorceress, and both of us reach
    into
all of that which is before us and all, that will come after.

   Inara Cedrins

BUT I DARE NOT WITHDRAW . . .

But I dare not withdraw my shoulder
as my shoulder supports your hand
as your hand may drop and get severed
and hitting the ground meet its death
as a rope from the tree of heaven
may loop as a noose round your neck
and perhaps it is only your hand
which is resting upon my shoulder
that gives you an ultimate hold on the earth.

   Ruth Speirs

DIDN'T YOU STOP . . .

Didn't you stop by the window
on purpose?
Didn't you specially want me
to notice?

Didn't you contemplate something
you'd do to me?

When a sulphur match strikes against sulphur
the outcome is light.

   Ruth Speirs

I CHARGED INTO THE UNDERGROWTH . . .

I charged into the undergrowth,
and on the lacquer of my car
the hazel leaf's green heart
lay flattened in the morning dew.

In Nature's bosom, ah,
the purity of dawns!

"Don't talk of bosom,"
the uprooted tree-trunk said to me,
"you've plunged into her very bowels
like a knife
doing hara-kiri."

What hara-kiri?
On the lacquer of my car,
the leaf's green heart.

What does it matter
if it beats no more?

   Ruth Speirs

AUTUMN COOLNESS

Today nature looks inward.

The frozen sparrow—
inward,
to warmth that still is there.

The saucepan
looks at the soup
in an unheated kitchen.

The clearing
through scruffy stubble
looks at the green beard
it'll erect to the skies next year.

Shrivelled fat
tries to see the place
where it once held
lean meat.

I gaze into myself:
how microscopic
and diffused
undone obligations become.
Worlds rush by
and look backward at mirror reflections—
won't there be an atomic reaction
if in the creating
that tremendous strength goes out
that goes into killing?

And one seed
looks inward
and trembles—
what will I be—
trash,
tree,
flower,

person,
non-person,
person,
non-person,
person,
non-person . . .

Inara Cedrins

SUNDAY

I go on tiptoe
through my city—
through a dead orchestra.

That little wooden house,
dry and brown
like a violin,
of what can it think without strings?

Through two houses,
through drums
I squeeze by
and fear in vain—
they don't thunder me to the ground,
for in each is an open window.

The shattered hole of Sunday.

And then
I can no longer escape—
in a shuffling gait
with empty eyes,
limp hands,
come the dead orchestra's musicians,

ours
and the children of noise.

At once they'll come up
from front and back
and ask to be allowed to smoke.

I won't scream.
They are children of noise.
But I am noise's father.

Inara Cedrins

HORSE DREAM

If one is judged by one's dreams,
prison is certain for me—
last night I led a horse
up onto St. Peter's tower
and said:
"Look, how I live!"

"It's nothing much,"
answered the horse,
"Though there are many tangles;
and, do you know what,
you'd better hobble me
for sometimes I start to fly.

The more you hobble,
the less tangles will remain."

I grew thoughtful.
"No, but look, horse,
look, where I live!"

"I'm looking—"
said the horse,

"But stables don't determine a soul's color.
I am a simple animal
when I stand,
and a horse, when I plow."

. . . I hobbled the horse
and grazed it
by the planetarium
all night.

And all night
the stars bit me.

A couple passed,
and the boy said seriously to the girl:
"That's the fashion nowadays."

Inara Cedrins

ASTER, BEGINNING IN PEONY

Broke off a peony. Put it in water.
With difficulty
a bumblebee banged at the pane,
to be given back its taken-away autumn.
With difficulty
can the broken-off be given back.
Difficult
to understand at once all bumblebees,
difficult to hold the world in one's chest,
when the leavetaking swallows
draw, like needles black and nimble,
your nerves out of you like strings
and veins like worsted.
Mists.
Those autumn mists are pitiless
when summer's memories smoke like a wreath

and, not letting you go, put you in Riga
with grey cloud peonies
ıp on steeples.

    Inara Cedrins

BLACK BEE

In a black, black pitch night
the shot lost its track,
flew as black through black,
like a black bee through the darkness,
parched for red honey,
seeking red honey.

I stood before the street door—
now you'll get red honey
only through my build!

Stand yourselves, brothers,
before all the street doors;
having drunk no red honey
the black bee in pitch night
will explode, whispering in the snow.

    Inara Cedrins

DON'T CRY

Don't cry.
You wash the spruces from my precipices.
It's enough.
For long now the stream's been full of snags.
In it the disc of the full moon
shatters.
The boys nutting on the shore

are afraid
to swim in the depths of my snags.
Don't cry.
Not yet.

Inara Cedrins

BUTTERFLY WEDDING

Above little flowers
and huge flowers
there's a butterfly wedding.

With a honey banquet,
strewn with golden flour,
there's a great wedding,
there's a good wedding.

The skies' moisture stands still
and doesn't come down.

Autumn stops
and—wonder is in its face.

Don't they feel,
that wedding throng,
how little of the dance there'll be,
how short the pleasure?

No, they don't feel it
in the slightest—
over them flows
only the wedding.

Let it be so always
in the old world—
no sorrow
where there's a wedding,
where there's marriage.

Ojārs Vācietis   137

No burials
of which children are born.

What dizzying wedding guests.
How they celebrate!

Inara Cedrins

CLOUDS

Don't push
porcelain clouds
into my sky!

Sight will believe
and be killed
on those slick hills.

My lightning
will crave
that white roundness,
will want to run it through
and will arrive deceived
at coldness.

It'll become angry
and strike
the cold
beauty.

Sharp fragments will rain,
drifting
into a summer's winter,
and when my children
with bare feet . . .

Inara Cedrins

LIGHTNING DRAWS

Lightning draws
leaf veins,
fills those in
with cloudflesh,
and that live, heavy leaf
lies over me—
to frighten me,
to guard
me.

Lightning draws
a sketch of a house
with sharp cornices,
steep roof
modern
curved
house walls—
there'll live
my heart,
an oval
and circle
worshipper.

Lightning draws
my feelings,
my thoughts'
seismograph
with high points,
deep gorges
without bottom
that fall away
somewhere
just beyond the horizon,
sketches briefly—

an eye-blink
lightning fragment.

My love,
bright,
short-lived—
lightning draws
your fragment.

Inara Cedrins

WHAT CHILDHOOD IS TO US

Sweet, distant
as yet uncooled tea
with the as yet unvisited
southern country's lemon.

And again—
a live, leaping into life parachutist,
dandelion floss
on the wind.

Yet in the windy, dark evening
when trees get goosebumps
in a frost,
when the heart wraps itself
in a painful hoop—
childhood to us is
that distant, white-glowing bit of kindling
at which we sat down
to invent electricity.

Inara Cedrins

OLGA LISOVSKA   1928–

Olga Lisovska has published several volumes of poetry and is much appreciated by both Soviet Latvian literati and the public for her lyrical, low-keyed poetry. She has translated many Russian authors and Langston Hughes. Lisovska contributes reviews and critical essays to leading literary periodicals and has been editor of a number of anthologies.

THE FOREST GEESE

The forest geese gather in flocks.
The brook freezes at night. It's time.
Alone with the clouds till morning hangs
the moon's half-emaciated cheek.

All night the drawn out wailing
cries of geese shiver over the brook.
The heart, like a mongrel, though generously fed,
ashamed,
yet readies itself too . . .

   Inara Cedrins

RIVERS DRIED

Rivers dried to the point of drought.
The time of rain drew out long.
Seven pages
are taken up by the Seven Year War.

Across the depths of centuries
stretches the naked bridge of history.
Forgotten, who loved who.
Remaining—the tribe humanity.

And, so it should not run barefoot
without birds in the trees, lacking;
each feels alone his strayings, tears,
and sings along only in the refrain.

Inara Cedrins

APPLES

There was a strong wind in the night.
        From the cold grass
you gather apples still wet with dew.
They're fragrant of other autumns in your palms,
of autumns that don't stop smarting the heart.

With clear red apples a blonde boy once ran,
tossing them through the window to a friend,
and was embarrassed and happy when the girl laughed,
smoothing the dewy apples against her cheek.

With brilliant apples he was accompanied away.
The road winds long over the backs of hills.
What was nurtured in one's breast, what was warmly desired,
all suddenly drew to a halt half said . . .
                    War.

And perhaps that's why an empty place stays in the heart,

so that in some way a year is called back through the years,
because the boy who tossed an apple to you once
will never again be met.

They lie wet and transparent in the cold grass,
but the dew doesn't smother their honeyed scent.
They're fragrant of other autumns in your palms,
shaken off too soon . . .
        There was a strong wind in the night.

   Inara Cedrins

CALM

Calm. It's black boats
drawn up on the shore of an evening.
Weariness, fading slowly,
faint ache in the hands.
Calm—it's the glow in the window.
Calm—it's the window in the afterglow.
Frozen in its stand against the sea,
a tree.
Calm. It's wild parsley,
sharply and strongly perfumed.
And in depressions of grass
the grasshoppers' song sounds.
Calm. It's—kettle and fire.
Drinking birch bark tea;
heavy steps beyond the window,
your hand
opening the door.

   Inara Cedrins

SMOKE BLOWS WHITE

Smoke blows white. Like a flag
on the black shaft of chimney.
Bread on the table. And the soul
guarded.

Smoke blows white. Like a flag.
Weaves warmly off into the air.
Is it of peace or restlessness
the soul's more easily reft?

Come across the white dew.
Put your hand in mine.
I'll not believe
this could be surrender.

  Inara Cedrins

THE DREAM

Pure as yet, and unguarded
like a naked fledgling
a dream was born in its nest—
and what scares me most about it
is that after its greatness and goodness
a person small and evil
with soiled hands, could grasp it
and not understand where to place it.

  Inara Cedrins

MY CHILDHOOD

1

My childhood—red clog sandals.
A long lineup of produce wagons.
And beyond that the forest—and, so they said—
beyond the forest, war.

A black locomotive pulled the grey wagons,
pulled many, many people.
The green-garbed people in wagons played and sang beautifully,
threw airy kisses to girls.

The locomotive shudders. Goes on yet a step,
puffing with weariness,
as if soothing, as if comforting:
whoosh, whoosh, whoosh . . .

Eyes in the box of the wagon. Brown and blue.
How can they sing?
Don't they know that beyond that forest,
beyond that forest—is war?

And faces again, new and strange.
The wide box of the produce wagon.
So the forty-second and forty-third
and forty-fourth year.

My childhood in red clog sandals
runs down the incline under the bridge . . .
Black echelons rumble across it,
and not a single one comes back.

2

From the black locomotive, a mote flies . . .
Soon the first snow will probably arrive.
Gentle as a lullaby the music flows,
and streets fall asleep little by little.

Through the window floods the freshness of late autumn night,
somewhere solitary footsteps clatter.
Why remind oneself of those distant times?
Not much to speak of or write there!

. . . I wake with a numb heart in the night
and don't understand what is the matter.
But in dream I cut off the carbide wick
so the room wouldn't be so light.

Heaped carts drive into the edge of the forest.
Horses whinny in the darkness.
The last patrol . . . further . . . further . . .
Will not one turn back here?

Bored. Bored. Bored.
Toss the book shut.
But the market field comes to me in dream.
Prisoners of war sing.

I awake . . . Oh, it was all seeming!
Silence thuds in my ears.
The moon shines.
But a shadow so like the gallows
falls from the window square to the floor.

One mote from the locomotive grates for years,
a bare birch branch strikes the window.
On a strange forest's edge, in darkness, beneath cumbered wheels
I'm afraid.
I'm afraid to wake.

Inara Cedrins

WHEN YOU EMERGE

When you emerge with an empty dish
from the forest clearing—
your eyes are full of mushrooms,
dense with berries.

Of what use now is regret,
or wondering why you're so late—
life, my precious life,
look back!

Inara Cedrins

ABOUT THE LITTLE PRINCE

It's not that he crashed,
that he won't manage to return to us,
that only children and poets
know how to call him occasionally to earth.

It seems to me rather that to you and me
the shortness of the moment is frightening.
But perhaps on his planet
time is measured differently?

Therefore one can't criticize his unpredictability,
or that he often can't be found.
The Little Prince isn't at fault.
He is good.
He'd come to everyone.

But everyone doesn't know how to be alone
and how not to fear sorrow;
to use the place where they stood yesterday, as comfort
for tomorrow.

Within one moment, while a white stork with long legs
soars over the field,

Olga Lisovska   147

for what a long time, bent by one gust of the wind,
two dandelions converse . . .

It's not true that such moments
are known only by children and poets.
He'll come to you once too.
Come.
And accustom you.

   Inara Cedrins

SIGNS

Signs, carved into wood,
tell where the path is to be found.
The sea, with amber in its hand,
rolls onto the shore for centuries.

Scrolls and parchment
remain, when cities fall to ruin.
Someone had toiled there before us,
so that the way wouldn't be lost . . .

Smoky cement carcass,
hundreds of neon stringers—
will the next century forget
or guard you?

Let's leave precise signs
to those who will follow in our footsteps;
the age will be pieced together, glued,
gathered in pluses and minuses—

let's leave precise signs!

   Inara Cedrins

DANGER DE MORT

France 1969

Grass grows easily.
Grass grows quickly.
Grass grows out during one summer
and doesn't recall
that before it was . . .
Grass grows easily.
Grass grows quickly,
green, green as December in Normandy.

   and grass climbs and stretches over half-demolished
   bunkers lying among rusted barbed wire
   where on a slanting piece of board the faded warning
   states "Danger de Mort!" but you don't question
   anything for the grass knows only one summer's tears and
   laughter
   the memory of grass is so short and wonderfully light

A tree grows much longer.
A tree grows with more difficulty,
and, when a grenade
splits the trunk
the tree feels it in its roots.
Ask, oh ask
those stumps
who once were called
purple-red maples . . .

   for roots still have to remember roots still have to hear that
   day when all the seacoast sounded like one shout in
   unison "Danger de Mort!" when in this hollow were
   death encamped and the celebratory banquets

but also the tree roots don't know how to scream out over the
    channel
like swallows . . .

Memory grows over the slowest.
Memory grows over with the most difficulty.
Memory is stubborn
against the balance of years,
the mortality of rain, hail and wind
and war . . .
Memory grows over the slowest,
but memory too
has only the length of life of a person.

    for only so long as smile wrinkles are embedded behind memory
                        on the cheek,
    while one hand in the world remembers
    the warmth of another in some eternal distant evening
    under purple-red maples

        for so long oh for so long this inscription won't be only
        inscription alone on a slanting board
        "Danger de Mort!"

Inara Cedrins

IMANTS ZIEDONIS 1933–

Imants Ziedonis, by critical and popular consensus, is the dean of Soviet Latvian poets. He was born near Riga into a family of fishermen, and earned a degree in philology at the Latvian State University as an evening school student while working. His first volume of poetry was published in 1956, and more than a dozen have followed. Among his citations and prizes is the title of People's Poet of Latvia. The poetry of Ziedonis has been translated into many languages and has been adapted for stage presentation. He is known for his children's poetry, and has written philosophical meditations, critical essays, and film scenarios. Ziedonis is also well known as a translator. He frequently travels abroad and has visited the United States.

THROUGH EVENING TWILIGHT

Through evening twilight,
through cool evening mists
we pass
and gradually become shadow.

We pass.
And no one any longer sees our profile.
There remains only a sense
that someone has gone by somewhere.

As though a door has creaked.
As though a rustling leaf has flown up.

As though some sorcerer
wanted to patch your heart.

As though from the summits had flown
the last flocks of leaves.
Someone wanted to caress you,
but passed . . .
and did not touch.

Inara Cedrins

SUCH A FINE HUM

such a fine hum in my ears
of thunder   of splitting stone
ear has to be placed against cannon
to hear

completely silent wheels pass over the cobblestones
even the wind is unfelt—I'm deafened
not hearing Everest avalanching
only the tarnishing of brooches is heard

Inara Cedrins

MY INSCRIPTIONS

my inscriptions on the window, which will fall
out onto the stocking heel—where it wears thin fastest;
out onto snowdrift—I am the drying kiln
having only so much as fire's flicker upon my face

so much as the creaking of gate, the rustle of paper
as spark falling into straw—so much I am

I go hunting but my heart's not in it
being a great believer in ash, believer in smoke
and a tiny droplet upon heated stone

    Inara Cedrins

WHEN CATS

(For Imants Kalnins)

When cats with black stripes yowl in the night
we are again unsure what we are.
And whether we should stand about the streets here
                           under the lindens,
or meet and multiply at doorways.

Or on stairs. Or at table. Or in chandeliers,
fastening our feet like candles
and burning, while the smallest flame still flickers,
till morning's brilliance dawns as executioner.

I don't know, old man, but in such nights
you'd better not lie down, and don't fall asleep—
for in torn black-striped catskins
our souls are yowling there under the stairs.

    Inara Cedrins

WE UNCOVERED A MYSTERY

We uncovered a mystery. We slowly
drew back the veil from its face—there
it lay, an unspecified form, overdue and
precipitate, clearly beyond comprehension,

with something concealed at its core;
and we felt quite certain that this was a
mystery and, as such, it had to be probed
and uncovered: with great care we drew
back its veil, and now it appeared before
us, a genuine mystery—not paid for, nor
ever encountered—and gleamed like
firewood which was soon to burn, and we
certainly wanted an insight and wanted to
know; we drew back its coverings, and
uncovered the mystery: crosswise, it lay
like a breeze that was lost, and there was
no knowing if it was weighty or merely
pretended to be so; or if it indeed was a
mystery; if it was, though, we had to uncover
it; eager, all eyes, we uncovered the
mystery: it now was at last a genuine and
more than genuine mystery, alarmingly
small and becoming still smaller and
smaller, and seemingly farther and farther
away, and we feared we might lose the
mystery, and no longer wished to uncover
it.
We were left with strange veils in our
hands. Like proof of our wish to uncover
something or other.

Ruth Speirs

MAY

This spring arrived as fresh
as guests, and we were almost ashamed
that we still wore our work clothes
and our hands weren't washed, and in the yard

the seedy-looking dog was shedding its winter coat.
And it was hard to figure who was at fault—
we or it: who came so out of turn.

Beauty, the old scholar said,
must come out of turn
and must create a slightly uneasy sensation.

Inara Cedrins

AUGUST

evening like a frog
sunlit
skin over the canal
green and blessed

pick up an apple
take a stone
everything speaks
of ancestral earth

vast distances
from the skylark in air
to the mouse in the granary
to the suckling pig in a sack

a great closeness
quietly maternal
green and full
and hunched over

sauna evening
connection through spirit
and such desire for the sake of everything
that I do right

Inara Cedrins

FALL WHEN STILL SHINING . . .

Fall when still shining! Or later it won't be believed
that you once were a star.
Go before you're burnt out.
Many sources of light in the skies burn out at their
preordained time, unobserved. But the sight of a falling star
prompts a wish for good fortune, the sight of a falling star . . .
Go, star, go in good time!
The time for you, star, is before it is time.
That is the time of a falling star.
Don't be late!
Touch glasses and, with that crystal sound in the air, be gone.

Ruth Speirs

I LOVE AN APPLE

I love an apple in the night, that floats
without any branch and without any tree.
I love an apple tree in night, that floats,
bending its branches in the dark, without roots.

And the whole earth that floats in night
is not erected nor propped by anything.
I love darkness that will not disappear
when I rise again tomorrow morning.

But will stand away, unseen,
and near when the sun sets.
I see a person, approaching now,
come from darkness, to go again into the dark.

Inara Cedrins

156   Imants Ziedonis

SMALL WINDOW

small window of the sauna
and wormhole in mushroom
and the tunnel into which the mountain train vanishes

how I long for home!
to go still deeper
and find the old beer drinkers
who I've not been with so long, long

small window of the sauna
and the hole made by mice in the chaff
and the tunnel into which the mountain train vanishes

Inara Cedrins

FIRST

First, when I switch on the light
I see my pencil's end.
In what strength does it live?
How does it see the hurdles while leaping?

White page like a bog—
tundra, in which one vanishes.
How does it find a place to hold on—
those tiny words?

A dog skims over the bog,
over the white page.
When I went there alone
I met nothing.

Inara Cedrins

TRY TO FIND

try to find
a neutral apple

they've all struggled heavily
against the heavy earth
and have fallen heavily

those green grafted branches
are witness
that a neutral apple
isn't possible

Inara Cedrins

THAT'S ONLY A RATTLING OF SHELL

That's only a rattling of shell
against other shells. The kernel isn't touched.
Oh, the deaf-mute too shows something with his hands.
So something in me, ten times suppressed,

lies fallen upon its mouth as though in moss.
Lies as though in mud. I can't get near.
And my tongue will again say something,
but that—I won't be able to express.

I lock the door behind me. Home
I am. Alone. And unprecedented silence.
Now that in me which found no expression, speaks.
Now speaks, when my tongue is silent.

Inara Cedrins

THE MOON SHINES

The moon shines behind the windowpane
as though through empty bottles.
Let's go by way of the moon's rays
as if by long noodles.

Tonight, grey cubes
have fallen into sleep here.
How I long to meet someone
who raises wild orchids!

Going by way of a moon ray . . .
Everything that you promise me
I would now give back
for one wild orchid.

Where night begins
and day disappears,
could there be found
a wild orchid existence?

Night that tears me,
night that rules me—
couldn't you be
a white fragrance of wild orchid,

raining my eyes full,
drizzling over mouth and forehead,
that I might fall asleep
quiet, peaceful.

Let grow in each eye
a little wild orchid seedling:
and I fall asleep quiet
and untorn.

Inara Cedrins

DON'T EAT

Don't eat while a song is being sung, my child! Never ever eat while a song is being sung, my little child! There is a tiny soul in that song, and maybe at this moment it is hungry. Don't eat while a song is being sung, my child.

Don't drink while a song is being sung, my child. A yellow thrush is pleading for rain, begging dew from the leaves. A thrush is begging, singing, not having eaten, not having drunk.

My child, we are a nation of eaters, but put your spoon down in your bowl while a song is being sung, my little child. Don't look at that man eating, don't learn from him. He has eaten all his songs. He can't tell the difference between songs and lettuce.

There is one door for both the spoon and the song. Does the spoon stop at the mouth when the song comes out singing? Take your spoon by the hand, my child, and lead it aside. Let the song pass first, my little child . . .

Juris Rozītis

I GROW RIPE

I grow ripe only in proximity. I ripen when there is something next to me. The presence of flowers makes me more contented. The presence of tall trees makes life safer, whereas small saplings awaken my paternal instincts. I want children. When the hazel is in blossom, I say: "Stop fooling around or you'll get a thrashing." When the bird-cherry feels a bit dizzy toward evening, I say: "You're not going anywhere. You've grown quite silly, running around in a daze. You should be studying for your final exams this spring." I see a young oak, and immediately remember that I have to buy shoelaces for my son.

Whenever there are heavy objects present, I feel that I am maturing. There is a rock standing next to me. He helps me to

160   Imants Ziedonis

grow. There is a stone on my breakfast table, next to my coffee cup. There is a stone on my desk, next to my canary. I take a stone with me on business trips. I pack it in a suitcase and take it with me.

Whenever someone is frying pancakes nearby, I feel that I am growing. I need fire in the oven. That's where my mother is busily working.

My father should always carry a box of matches in his pocket. The eternal flame should always burn in the Cemetery of the Brethren.

Let's go to a tower. Gate towers, armory towers, bell towers. The winds that howl in their windows have never howled through your hair. You'll never raise your arm so high, and you'll never smell the smells of heaven. When a tower raises its hat of a morning, greeting me, I feel as happy as a child. He must have seen something in me.

I grow ripe when there is something next to me. One Sunday in every month the Armory Tower stands next to me, and cannons grow in me.

One Sunday in every month gate towers stand next to me, and I allow prisoners to escape.

One Sunday in every month a bell tower stands next to me. Clouds grow in the sky, the wind hums in the bells, and I can't say a word.

Juris Rozītis

PRAYER

You, huge evening sun,
You, who stand above fishermen,
You stand above people's lives
and fishes' deaths.

You, huge evening sun,
In whose light the horizon's air burns,
Give to my fishermen
Their daily bread.

Show them the ways of fish:
There, in depths of the sea current,
Swims all their wealth,
Tangible and tasteful.

Their motorcycles swim,
Cherry and apple seedlings . . .
You, huge evening sun,
Show them the ways of fish!

But—above all—give fruitful wives.
Wives with burgeoning bellies!
You, huge evening sun,
Help sons to be born.

Help one son to be born
rather than a hundred transistors.
Help the people, sun,
Help us in this matter!

Inara Cedrins

A LITTLE SHIP

A little ship is sinking in me. Another one sinks. My heart is
heavy. My heart beats between sunken ships.

For me they were beautiful ships. And they still are beautiful
amongst the crabs.

. . . this one was too eager. It drew barges; it had enough strength
for nine barges, but always hooked a tenth on.

. . . this one sank because of its friends. Because of its friends'
tastes. A dolphin appeared over the left gunwale wearing mattress-

162   Imants Ziedonis

ticking trousers. Everyone rushed to the left gunwale. On the right side a sea cow appeared, wearing eye shadow (a rare phenomenon) and everyone rushed to the right gunwale, and capsized the little ship.

. . . this one sank because of her. "Won't my ship go any faster?" I knew it couldn't go any faster, but I poured more oil into the furnace. The furnace blew up into the sky, and is still circling around Venus.

. . . and this one just sank through pure pagan joy. On Midsummer Eve I set fire to it, and it burnt to the waterline, and went down hissing.

Life passed—sinking ships.

I never gave a thought to my heart. Every now and again it gives a flutter. There's nothing wrong with it, only . . . probably a ship's mast pressing against it, and there is no one down there to help it.

Wandering around ships' decks and saloons, I never once gave thought to submarines. Now I'm stuck without first aid.

The only hope for help is from foreign submarines.

I'm building my own, but it's quite possible I won't manage it.

Juris Rozītis

BRIDGE FEELING

Bridge feeling. Walking on water. Walking on a moonbeam, on a road of light in the water. Walking on ripples, on sheets of ice, on the wind's glitter on the surface of the water. Ducks fly over. Bees fly over. At night, bats. I walk across.

I believe it is possible to walk on reflections. On reflections of fir trees, irises, and oak trees in the river. I walk across on your reflection.

Your "Come here" like a reflection. Your arm raised in greeting falls across the river, right up to my hazel bush.

The glow of your campfire on your tent casts a reflection across the river. Someone calls "Come" from the other shore. Is that a voice or an echo?

Try doubting halfway over. Many have drowned like that. Shadows and reflections and whispers. The river—now seems frozen over, now not frozen over. Now there's a sturdy footbridge, now a road of light in the water. (Hey! Someone's calling you!) Is it over? Now it seems to be over, now it seems not to be over. Sort of like a shout of joy, sort of like a cry for help.

So one person goes to another. And no one knows if he's made it over. No one to ask. One went, and didn't make it. Another believed and made it across. Both went along the same reflection in the water, one went to Heaven, the other went to Hell, along the very same "Come here."

Whoever walks on wooden and reinforced concrete bridges, goes away and comes back—high up over the river. Whoever walks on reflections, on shadows, on the scent of bird cherries in the river, never comes back. No one knows whether they go or not.

All that remains is their cry of joy or fear across the waters.

No bridge leads to a person.

The only way to reach a person is across reflections.

Juris Rozītis

SOMETIMES I FEEL

Sometimes I feel that God is practising football,* using me as the ball. He swings his leg back, and kicks me in the ribs (as much as God can kick at all!). And I have no idea where His goals are. And I

*Soccer.

164   Imants Ziedonis

have no idea whom He is playing against. If He wanted to pass, He could kick me to the Devil, or to Firsov, or to Pelé, or to the boy in the backyard. But no, He just plays by Himself. The Archangel Michael is standing in the goals, but God doesn't kick me towards the goal, because then I might roll out into the world. God would never stoop so low as to play with mortals. And so He passes, kicks, and drops me in the celestial flowerbed, until next time. Boring! Flowers all around me—"apples of Paradise," blue hops like anemones. But in my dreams I see a whole stadium roaring, and a goalkeeper with a broken leg. Here the flowers aren't even manured. They grow through the grace of God. Here there isn't even a puddle for a ball to fall into and to wallow in like a pig. What a temptation—if only God would really swing back His leg, and kick me with all His might at the angel's white underwing. Like marmalade into tissue paper!

He kicks me with His bare feet, of course. God could never break a toe! But now I wish He had real football boots, and someone else to play with. But no. God plays alone. Stubbornly and consistently alone. God's football is a very lonely game. We are both lonely. God is lonely, but this football of His is lonelier still. No out-of-bounds, no penalty kick, no scuffling in the goal square. Nothing.

As for rugby—they don't know anything about it in Heaven.

Juris Rozītis

FISH ROT

Fish rot starting from the head. The triumphant rot sets in in the morning. You wake up like pancake dough spilt all over the bed. You should get up, you should get ready for the start, but the starting line wasn't drawn last night. You'll have to do it this morning. The only thing is—the chalk's missing.

You'll have to look for the chalk. The only thing is—you dropped it somewhere last night. You'll make do with a piece of charcoal.

Your starting slippers should be by the bed, but you left them near

Imants Ziedonis   165

the finishing line last night. Your shoelaces are broken, you'll have to find—maybe even buy—new ones. (The correct time—nine thirty precisely, nine thirty precisely.)

Either the starting pistol has lost its voice, or else I didn't hear it, and all the others have already run off. (The correct time—nine thirty-five precisely.)

Yesterday's hairs are still stuck in the comb. Where to put them? The waste basket is full to overflowing. You'll have to take the garbage out. The early bird catches the worm. (The correct time—nine fifty precisely, nine fifty precisely.)

And then you'll have to boil the water for coffee. No, first you'll have to clear the table.

Ten o'clock already! At which kilometer mark are they by now? Spikes hoeing the running track. We athletes are the farmers of the running track—ploughers, hoers, carrot cultivators. Our legs are like those sharp, fanged couch-grass hoes. What a feeling when your running spikes dig into the ground! Like the prongs of an electric plug thrust into a wall socket. You're plugged into the electric mains, and the tingle begins to climb from the soles of your feet, up through your calves. (The correct time—ten thirty precisely. Half past ten!) What's happening to me this morning? The room is full of yesterday's germs. Last night's invasion forces have landed this morning and are rubbing out the starting lines. Sawing through my sportsman's tendons. Last night's hole still in my sock. Last night a button came loose—I wonder why I didn't sew it on. The main thing now is to press my pants. The correct-time-keeper is no longer saying anything. I look at the clock—half past eleven!

I run out into the street, a sandwich in my mouth. The last few stragglers are just crossing the finishing line. The high jumpers are smoothing over the little pits in the sawdust. Weaklings with transistors are lounging around, but the starting pistol, having done its job, goes off to lunch.

My morning started to rot from the head.

Juris Rozītis

166   Imants Ziedonis

HAIRPINS

Morning. Waking on my shoulder,
Big blue eyes look up, serene.
On the table by the bedside
Are her hairpins—seventeen.

He who's seen them knows for certain
That their eyes can glow with spite
At the points of seventeen hairpins—
Eyes of devils, small and bright.

Sometimes I am seized by madness:
On the stage and on the screen
There are actresses with hairpins
Facing me in every scene.

In the night those jealous devils
Prod and shake me: "Have you seen
What this is? It is her hairpin.
Do you know where she has been?"

Winter. I'll protect the roses,
Strewing fir twigs all around,
And I'll peg the stems of roses
With her hairpins to the ground.

I'll grow old. An ancient, battered
Hat will flop about my face.
Mumbling still about her hairpins,
Toothless, useless, there I'll pace.

I shall say: "The devil take you!"
When you talk of love, my friend.
Love, I tell you, is a poison
In a small black hairpin's bend.

Ruth Speirs

Imants Ziedonis   167

HOW THE CANDLE BURNS

How the candle burns.
How beautifully the candle burns!
What a white light gleams, swinging.
And darkness flees. And again—light flees.
And God and the Devil barter for my soul.

But the candle burns.
How beautifully the candle burns!
And the wind runs up and frightens my flame.
Paraffin runs over the candle's edges
as someone already awaits my passing.

But the candle burns.
How whitely the candle burns!
And darkness bows its full head in wonder:
from beginning to end it burns whitely
till the wick slowly drowns in paraffin.

But something dims—
yet something lightly grows dimmer.
Still in my eyes the candle's light glimmers.
But before me stands the skies' great market
where God and the Devil barter candle souls.

Inara Cedrins

SOURCES

LINARDS TAUNS
Exeter Books chapbook No. 17, trans. Ruth Speirs 1969; *The Literary Review*

ASTRĪDE IVASKA
Ziemas tiesa [Winter Judgement], 1968, The River Hill Press, Shippenville, Pennsylvania; *Solis silos* [A Step into the Forest], 1973, Daugava, Sweden; *Ezera kristības* [The Lake's Christening], 1966, The River Hill Press, Shippenville, Pennsylvania; *Līču loki* [Curving Bays], 1981, Daugava, Sweden; *Gaisma ievainoja (The Light Wounded)*, 1982, Daugava, Sweden

GUNĀRS SALIŅŠ
Melnā saule [Black Sun], 1967, Grāmatu Draugs, New York; Exeter Books chapbook No. 17; *The Literary Review*

BAIBA BIČOLE
Buŗot [To Cast Spells], 1976, Grāmatu Draugs, New York; *Griežos* [I Turn], 1981, Grāmatu Draugs, New York

OLAFS STUMBRS
Etīdes [Etudes], 1964, Alfred Kalnājs, Chicago; *Vāveres Stunda* [Squirrel Hour], 1970, Ceļinieks, Ann Arbor, Michigan; *Daudz laimes u.t.t.* [Much luck and so forth], 1970, Leon Rumaks Bookseller, New York

AINA KRAUJIETE
Kristalls un māls [Crystal and Clay], 1976, Daugava, Sweden; *Ne bungas ne trompetes* [Not Drums Nor Trumpets], 1974, Grāmatu Draugs, New York; *No aizpirktās paradīzes* [From A Bartered Paradise], 1966, The River Hill Press, Shippenville, Pennsylvania; *Es esmu vasara* [I Am Summer], 1963, The River Hill Press, Shippenville, Pennsylvania

VIZMA BELŠEVICA
Kamola tinēja [The Winder of Yarn], 1981, Liesma, Riga; *Gadu gredzeni* [The Rings of Years], 1969, Liesma, Riga; *Madarās* (Madders), 1976, Liesma, Riga; *Jūra deg* [The Sea Burns], 1966, Liesma, Riga

MĀRIS ČAKLAIS

Sastrēgumstunda [Obstruction Hour], 1974, Liesma, Riga; *Uz manām trepēm* [On My Stairs], 1979, Liesma, Riga; *Dzer avotu, celiniek* [Drink at the Well, Traveller], 1969, Liesma, Riga

ĀRIJA ELKSNE

Stari [Rays], 1982, Liesma, Riga; *Mājupceļš* [The Road Home], 1978, Liesma, Riga

OJĀRS VĀCIETIS

Gamma [Gamma], 1976, Liesma, Riga; *Antracīts* [Anthracite], 1978, Liesma, Riga; *Zibens pareizrakstība* [Lightning Spelling], 1980, Liesma, Riga

OLGA LISOVSKA

Stārķu krasts [The Storks' Shore], 1978, Liesma, Riga

IMANTS ZIEDONIS

Caurvējš [A Draft], 1975, Liesma, Riga; *Epifānijas* [Epiphanies], 1978, Liesma, Riga; *Poēma par pienu* [Poem About Milk], 1977, Liesma, Riga; *Man labvēlīgā tumsā* [The Well-meaning Darkness], 1979, Liesma, Riga; *Kā svece deg* [How the Candle Burns], 1971, Liesma, Riga